Discovering Timothy, Titus and Philemon

THE GUIDEPOSTS HOME BIBLE STUDY PROGRAM

Floyd W. Thatcher   *General Editor*
Robin White Goode   *Associate Editor*
Bob E. Patterson   *Technical Consultant*

EDITORIAL ADVISORY BOARD

The Epistles of Paul the Apostle to
TIMOTHY, TITUS AND PHILEMON

Discovering Timothy, Titus and Philemon   James Williamson
What This Scripture Means to Me   Katy Stokes
Photographs   William S. LaSor
Book Design   Elizabeth Woll
Cover Artist   Ben Wolhberg

DISCOVERING TIMOTHY, TITUS AND PHILEMON

The Guideposts
Home Bible Study Program

GUIDEPOSTS

Carmel   New York   10512

THE GUIDEPOSTS HOME BIBLE STUDY PROGRAM
The Epistles of Paul to Timothy, Titus and Philemon:
    1. DISCOVERING TIMOTHY, TITUS AND PHILEMON
    2. My Working Bible
    3. Knowing More About Timothy, Titus and Philemon

Contents

How to Use the Guideposts Home Bible Study Program

1. Read the passages in your *Working Bible* that are included in the appropriate lesson material in *Discovering Timothy, Titus and Philemon*. In the margins of your *Working Bible* jot down any notes you'd like to call special attention to.

2. Then, to amplify the Scriptures you've read, study Lesson 1 in *Discovering Timothy, Titus and Philemon*. As you read the lesson keep your *Working Bible* open so you can look up the many Scripture references that are included in the lesson.

3. When you complete each lesson, quiz yourself on what you've learned, with the quiz booklet, *Knowing More About Timothy, Titus and Philemon*.

Repeat this rhythm as you read each lesson, to get the most from your study of God's Word.

Publisher's Introduction

Our studies in this series of lessons give us our most intimate view into the heart and life of Paul, the apostle to the gentiles. And they are his most personal writings.

The two letters to Timothy and the letter to Titus were addressed to two old friends—men who had traveled widely with him and who had had the benefit of his personal attention and training.

The Timothy letters are characterized by a unique warmth because Paul sees his young friend as his son in the Lord. As Paul counsels Timothy on practical Christian living and teaching and church organization, the tone is that of a mentor deeply interested in the progress of his protégé.

The Letters to Timothy.

The first letter to Timothy is rich in practical guidance for Christian living and also contains instruction on the development of organization and leadership in the church community.

In the second letter to Timothy it is likely that we have the last words Paul wrote before his death. The emphasis here is on being loyal and faithful to the true gospel, avoiding useless controversy, and the importance of Christian discipline in personal and church life.

Paul's sensitive nature and caring concern are seen vividly in these two letters. He knows so well the temptations and dangers that confronted his Christian friends in their pagan Roman setting. But in his counsel and warnings we find no judgmental or critical overtones. Instead we find a Paul who urges faithfulness to sound doctrine and right relationships based on God's grace.

The Letter to Titus.

This short letter was written to Titus, one of Paul's converts and a frequent traveling companion, and the leader of the church in Crete. Here, as in the Timothy letters, there is a strong personal note along with practical instruction.

In our studies we get early insight into the particular difficulties Titus faced because of the character of the Cretan people, "The Cretians are alway liars, evil beasts, slow bellies [lazy and useless]" (Titus 1:12). The Roman world knew them as an undisciplined people.

While we don't know much about Titus, for Paul to have assigned him the task of shepherding the Cretan Christians indicates a strength of character and quality of Christian leadership. It was a tough assignment, and knowing Paul as we do, it is obvious he felt Titus was the man for the job.

In Titus, as in Timothy, practical advice is given on church organization and structure with special emphasis on the importance of order. The central theme, however, is sound teaching and the doing of good works, "This is a faithful saying, and these things I will that thou affirm constantly, that they which have believed in God might be careful *to maintain good works*" (Titus 3:8, italics mine).

From Paul's words in this valuable little letter we are reminded that it is right actions—good works—not just words that give validity to our faith.

The Letter to Philemon.

The shortest of Paul's letters—twenty-five verses—is often overlooked in Bible studies. But as we will see in Lesson 8, it offers rich insight into the heart and spirit of Paul as he communicates with one of his very close friends.

In this letter Paul pleads for his friend to have mercy on his runaway slave, who now returns as a Christian. But as we study it, we find helpful guidance on being a friend and having friends. We also confront the sometimes uncomfortable truth that all people are equal in God's sight. And if we've been inclined to think that the Apostle was indifferent to the social evil of slavery, we stand corrected as we get the full implications of the favor he is asking of Philemon.

Paul's letter to Philemon is proof positive of the truth he expressed earlier, "There is neither Jew nor Greek, there is neither bond nor free, there is neither male nor female: for ye are all one in Christ Jesus" (Gal. 3:28).

Preface

In these eight lessons we come now in our studies to four highly important letters credited to the Apostle Paul. These are unique in that they are directly addressed to a person instead of to a church or group of churches.

1 and 2 Timothy and Titus are commonly referred to as the Pastoral Epistles, having received this designation from a Bible scholar early in the eighteenth century. The designation is most appropriate because they were written by a chief pastor to pastors and leaders of local church congregations about the administration and daily life and work of the church.

The Pastoral Epistles.

At the time of the writing of these letters the early church was growing rapidly. The first-century Christians were only a heartbeat away from their earlier, pagan religious influence. False teaching was a constant problem in the young congregations. A focus of these letters was to combat especially the heresy of Gnosticism.

The Purpose of the Pastoral Epistles.

At the same time the rapid growth of the church soon made it necessary to devise an organization structure. In these letters Paul gives careful instruction for church leaders and for qualification for leadership.

When Were the Pastoral Letters Written?

The book of Acts closes with Paul confined to prison in Rome. Over the centuries there have been two views of what happened next. Certain of the early church fathers believed that Paul was released from his first confinement in Rome and made his long-anticipated missionary trip to Spain before retracing once again his travels in Greece and Asia Minor. It is then believed that he was rearrested and imprisoned again in Rome where he wrote the Pastoral Letters, knowing that his death was near.

However, most modern New Testament scholars do not accept this early idea and believe that Paul was confined in a Roman prison one time and sometime after Luke closed out the Acts account Paul was martyred for his faith. Such being the case, it is believed that these letters were written toward the close of that confinement.

Authorship of the Pastoral Letters.

While it isn't our purpose in these lessons to get tangled up in technical problems, we do want to alert you to opposing views as to authorship. Although the writer is clearly identified as Paul in the letters themselves, there have been and are New Testament scholars who feel that they may have been written by a student of Paul for several stylistic reasons.

And then, of course, there are those who accept Paul's authorship for equally good reasons. It is quite likely that a survey of New Testament scholars would reveal about an equal difference of opinion. The wording in the lessons that follow assumes Paul's authorship based on the wording of the text.

The important thing to us in our study is the practical teaching on the preparation for Christian living and leadership contained in these letters. Here, too, we gain valuable insights on the order and structure of the early church as a means of guidance in our twentieth-century church life.

The Letter to Philemon.

This, as you will see, is Paul's most personal letter and was written to an intimate friend, even though the Apostle asks that it also be read to the Lycus Valley Christian congregations in Colossae, Laodicea, and Hierapolis.

As we will see in our studies, its purpose was primarily to ask Philemon to accept his runaway slave who had found his way from Colossae to Rome on stolen money, but had then become a Christian under Paul's guidance. After that he became the apostle's close friend and helper.

While this is the shortest of Paul's letters, our study will reveal remarkable insights into the apostle's personal life and thought. From this letter we will gain inspiration for our own journey of faith as we are reminded that all people are brothers and sisters in Christ irrespective of race or social position.

LESSON 1
1 TIMOTHY 1–2

Advice to a Young Minister

Dear Father, Thank You for Your abundant grace, which alone saves and heals me. AMEN.

My Uncle Fred was a Presbyterian minister who had the rare distinction of serving one congregation for over forty years. When I was very young, I thought his clerical collar looked funny, and I had no idea what he did for a living. Our family saw him a couple of times a year, and we usually exchanged gifts at Christmas. But his children were several years older than my brothers and I were, so we were never very close.

When I grew older and felt the call to the ministry, I suddenly became more interested in Uncle Fred. I remember writing and asking him for counsel and advice. And I also remember how excited I was when I received his response. I opened the letter with eager anticipation and read every word many times. His words of wisdom then have been of help to me ever since.

From then on we corresponded regularly. My letters were full of questions, and his responses always contained helpful advice. Now and then he would send me copies of his favorite books—all of which I have treasured over the years. When he died, I felt a deep sense of loss, but I was grateful for his sage counsel over the years. His letters and advice have helped me to mold my own life and ministry.

I expect that Timothy felt much the same way when Paul took him under his wing and guided him in his pilgrimage of faith and service. What a privilege it was for Timothy to accompany Paul on some of his missionary journeys and to learn by listening to and watching the great apostle.

Throughout his training period Timothy grew in his knowledge of the Christian faith and matured as a witness and minister of the Lord. We get an early clue as to Paul's confidence in young Timothy when the apostle put him in charge of the church at Ephesus, a most important and significant assignment.

The Opening of the Letter.

In writing now to Timothy, Paul opens his letter according to first-century custom. Unlike today when we sign our names at the end of a letter, writers then began by identifying themselves, "Paul, an apostle of Jesus Christ by the commandment of God our Saviour, and Lord Jesus Christ, which is our hope" (1:1).

As you've noticed, I'm sure, Paul was always careful to identify himself as an apostle of Jesus Christ. This established his authority for writing as he did. At the same time, though, we know that Paul did not do this out of pride or arrogance, for as you will remember from an earlier study, he referred to himself as the "least of the apostles" (1 Cor. 15:9). He considered himself "the least" because of his persecution of Christians before his conversion. But he also knew that when Christ appeared to him on the Damascus road, he received a special call from God that led him out to the far corners of the Roman Empire with the Good News of salvation.

Next, we see in verse 1 that Paul refers to Christ as "our hope." This was an important description of the Savior for first-century Christians. Christ was indeed their hope—and ours—for living a faithful life in a hostile environment. He is our hope now, but He is also our hope for victory over death—He is our Resurrection hope. In Him, life takes on an authentic meaning and richness (John 10:10).

Addressed to Timothy.

Next, Paul writes that this letter is to Timothy. This, too, was standard practice in first-century letter writing. And he identifies Timothy as "my own son in the faith" (1:2).

Much speculation has arisen in an attempt to interpret this phrase.

Some interpreters have taken it to mean that Paul was the one who led Timothy to the Lord. But this idea seems inconsistent with Acts 16:1 where we meet Timothy for the first time in the New Testament. Here we are told that he was a disciple in Lystra in the province of Galatia, and that he had a good reputation among the Christians in the surrounding districts. And in another place Paul writes that Timothy's mother Eunice and his grandmother were faithful Christian models for him to follow (2 Tim. 1:5).

From all of this there seems little question but that Paul met Timothy on an early missionary journey—possibly his first. We do know, though, without any question that a strong bond was established on Paul's second visit to Lystra. And we know that the Apostle was strongly attracted to the young man because of his eagerness to grow in faith and serve the church (Acts 16). Then as the two men became more attached to each other, Paul began to feel about Timothy as a proud father would toward his son.

In most first-century letters the writer would have followed up his identification of the receiver with the salutation, "Greetings." But instead Paul concluded his introduction with a blessing, "Grace, mercy, and peace, from God our Father and Jesus Christ our Lord" (1:2). However, it is interesting that the Greek word for "greetings" is very similar to the word for "grace." So, by a very simple wordplay Paul transformed an ordinary letter into a special Christian message.

Next, Paul moves immediately into a matter of great concern to him. When leaving Ephesus for a visit to Macedonia, he had assigned Timothy the task of correcting certain false teachers who were polluting the church with their errant teachings. As we've already seen, a number of heresies assailed the early Christians, causing confusion in the church (1:3–4).

Evidently, the particular heresy plaguing the Ephesian church at this time had to do with, among other things, "fables"—idle stories—and "endless genealogies." Jewish culture had long been preoccupied with stories and genealogies. At the same time, first-century Greek culture was saturated with Gnosticism and its preoccupation with

Timothy's Special Assignment.

"secret knowledge" and speculation about the "questions" that plague the human race. You will remember, too, that the Gnostics believed matter and even the human body were evil and alienated from God. For them, liberation was only possible through the secret and special knowledge, which only they possessed. Obviously, Christianity was vigorously opposed to such false ideas because the grace of God is not limited to the intellectually elite, but is available to everyone.

Paul says clearly that the kind of fables involved in this "special" knowledge could only stir up trouble and cause confusion in the church. And he knew that if the church was to continue to grow, these false teachers would have to be stopped. The Good News of Jesus Christ is not something to be debated but is to be accepted by faith.

The End of the Commandment Is Charity.

Paul has more to say about the heresy later in the letter, but now he directs his attention toward the true teaching of the Good News—it isn't the possession of some kind of secret or mysterious knowledge, but in being driven and controlled by love. As Paul worded it here, "Now the end of the commandment is charity [love] out of a pure heart, and of a good conscience, and of faith unfeigned" (1:5).

You would know why Paul wrote that real Christian love comes from a pure heart and a good conscience if you had known my friend Mr. Smith. I was warned about him very soon after I began to work in a church during some of my college days.

Mr. Smith's wife Eloise was a member of the women's organization, a couple of Bible study classes, and several prayer groups. She was a valued church member and one of the nicest people I've ever met.

Now, while Mr. Smith did a lot of good things for the church, he never seemed to enjoy it. There was never a happy look on his face, and he always acted as if church was a waste of time. Whenever anyone asked him to a social event or to participate in a project, he made endless excuses—until either his conscience or his wife got to him. Only then would he give in, but he griped and complained all the way.

Mr. Smith did many fine things for the church, but I always had the feeling he did them solely from a sense of obligation. His acts of "charity" didn't seem to be motivated by love, a pure heart, and a good conscience.

Ruins at Troas. On Paul's second missionary journey young Timothy joined the apostle in Lystra and after visiting churches in Galatia they arrived at Troas on the northeastern coast of Asia. It was from this Aegean seaport city that Paul and Timothy and the rest of their party embarked for Macedonia. This was the beginning of the long association between Timothy and his mentor, Paul.

We've all known people, I'm sure, who are quite liberal with their acts of charity, but it is obvious their interest is primarily in what they will gain from their "generosity." And there are always those who seem to give to the church or various civic charities in order to attract attention and obtain prestigious and influential committee assignments.

On the other hand, pure-hearted love is much quieter

and often quite difficult to identify. It is frequently less public and free from either subtle or overt power plays.

I recall vividly discovering after my ordination service that a letter had been left for me at the church office. The writer expressed belief in me and encouraged me to continue in my spiritual growth. When I looked for the signature, I found these words, "Someone from the church." Accompanying the letter were copies of some loans I had taken out for school expenses—all marked, "Paid in Full." I have no idea who my benefactor was, but I'm sure his or her act of love came from a pure heart and a genuine commitment to Christ.

Paul's Judgment on False Motives.

It is clear from Paul's next words that there were those in the Ephesian church whose words and actions were not motivated by love, but who were involved in "vain janglings" (1:6). When the Apostle speaks of "vain janglings," he is referring, I believe, to the Gnostic heretics he mentioned in verse 4. Their fables and stories were no more than the shallow sound of a circus tambourine when compared with the life-changing Good News of Jesus Christ. Paul says that their knowledge is not the result of spiritual insight, for they understand "neither what they say, nor whereof they affirm" (1:7).

Paul then in verse 8 appears to be referring to another Gnostic aberration, which insisted that a person who has achieved the "goodness" that comes with secret and mysterious knowledge has passed beyond any need for the Law. Instead, his so-called "goodness" would dictate how he should behave. But Paul insists that even though true goodness comes from the heart, we are never beyond our need for the Law, for "the law is good, if a man use it lawfully" (1:8). It is not fear of the Law but love for God that motivates our behavior.

A List of Lawless Traits.

Paul moves on now to expand his comments on the Law by stating that its purpose is to bring judgment on those who violate it. And then he gives his readers a list of sins that are condemned by the Law (1:9–10).

As Paul sees it here, the Law is for those who rebel against God and are disobedient to His will. It is for those who are defiant and who have abandoned all regard for the truth. And it is for those who have no regard for human life and who are morally corrupt and perverted.

Then to make sure he hasn't missed anything Paul says that the Law is to judge and condemn "any other thing that is contrary to sound doctrine"—any word or action that violates the purity of the Good News.

In this list of lawless traits we get a vivid panoramic view of the sinfulness of the hostile environment in which the first-century Christians were trying to live holy lives. Paul knew and understood their struggle, and so he gives them these words of warning as he seeks to strengthen their faith in God's love.

At the same time there is a practical lesson here for us. Our world is rocked by brother fighting brother and the indiscriminate killing of innocent bystanders with car bombs. We are aware, too, of the times of flagrant disregard for truth in political, business, and social life, even as we see the spreading stain of moral laxity and the flaunting of sexual sins. Along with our first-century Christian brothers and sisters we find ourselves surrounded frequently with very little to remind us of love, a pure heart, or a good conscience. But that is only a part of the story, for over against all of that is the grace of God, which Paul had experienced vividly in his own life.

The Gospel Is a Sacred Trust.

For Paul, the answer to the lawlessness and sin that characterized first-century society was the grace of God. He knew it was God's grace that had confronted him on the Damascus road, and it is his understanding of that grace that comes through in this part of our lesson (1:11–14). In verse 11 he writes of "the glorious gospel of the blessed God, which was committed to my trust." And for Paul, the gospel of Jesus Christ was not something that could be received and then kept hidden. The life-changing news of salvation through Christ is meant to be shared both by our words and actions. Our salvation doesn't mature in isolation or by following certain rules or laws. Rather, it is to be lived out in daily life in fellowship with others.

The Apostle now continues his reflective thoughts as he thanks God for the privilege that is his in being given this trust, and being chosen and enabled by Christ to be His witness. His life and service for the Lord is something Paul took very seriously. And, while it is true Paul was singled out by God for a special task, we all share in his calling to be a witness for the Lord.

Too many of us have the idea that to be considered faithful enough to be entrusted with sharing the gospel means to be called to a specialized ordained ministry. Not so! Wherever you are, and whatever your gifts, talents, and calling, you can be a minister of the gospel—a witness to God's grace. Your service for Christ may not involve preaching sermons or teaching classes or administering churches or going to denominational meetings. But it does involve serving others as you would serve Christ Himself.

There is a story in the Gospel of Matthew that illustrates this point. It is about the great Judgment Day. In the story, all of humanity is separated into two groups—sheep and goats. The Lord told the sheep who had ministered to Him whenever they saw a need that they would "inherit the kingdom prepared for you from the foundation of the world." In response to their question as to when they had seen Him in need and ministered to Him, the Lord responded, "Inasmuch as ye have done it unto one of the least of these my brethren, ye have done it unto me" (Matt. 25:40).

From this we see that the measure or standard for judgment has nothing to do with sermons or great lesson plans or even regular attendance at church meetings. Jobs and professions are not even mentioned in the story. Instead, the standard for being faithful is in recognizing the needs of another person and then doing something to meet those needs. This is the gospel that has been entrusted to all of us.

Christ Came to Save Sinners.

The Apostle Paul felt very good about the ministry that he had been given by the Lord. He always believed that he would carry out his task faithfully. Yet he never lost sight of the fact that he was saved by the grace of God, not by his own goodness. He was a realist. He was keenly aware of his own shortcomings as he wrote, "Christ Jesus came into the world to save sinners; of whom I am chief" (1:15). He remembered well his days as a persecutor of the church and a hater of Christians. At the same time he remembered his confrontation with the risen Christ on the road to Damascus. It was God's saving and nurturing grace that had kept him steady from that day on in spite of his imperfection. And it was by God's grace that he realized he could fulfill whatever job God had for him. There was neither

24

arrogance nor false humility in Paul's awareness that in Christ he could accomplish anything.

So often we have a tendency to sell ourselves short. Intentionally or otherwise we cop out by telling ourselves that we do not have the talent to do a certain thing. So often in my church work I've heard someone say, "I'd love to teach a Sunday school class, but I'm just not good enough." Or, "I don't have the background," or, "I don't know the Bible well enough."

Actually, the greatest problem is not lack of skill as a teacher or lack of knowledge about the Bible. I've come to believe our most urgent need is to accept honestly the grace that God has offered us, and to permit ourselves to be "counted faithful" (1:12). The Good News is that God trusts us. He believes in us, and He has given each of us a mission in life. As Christians, our self-image is rooted in the awareness that God is with us. It is this reality that apparently overwhelms Paul now as he lifts his heart in praise through one of the most beautiful doxologies in all of the New Testament; "Now unto the King eternal, immortal, invisible, the only wise God, be honour and glory for ever and ever. Amen" (1:17).

After Paul's ecstatic parenthesis on God's grace and his own calling, he returns to the task at hand: to charge Timothy to continue in his own commitment to stop the false teachers, and to restore order within the Ephesian church (1:18–20).

Paul first reminds Timothy that he has support for his task. There were many people in Ephesus who were with him. He was not alone. He even reminds Timothy of some of the statements made about his potential for service as he commits this charge, "…according to the prophecies which went before on thee" (1:18). It is possible that these statements were made by church elders in his home as they watched him mature. Or possibly these were comments made at his ordination. Wherever they were made, the important thing was that Timothy was supported by people who believed in him.

Paul's words in verse 19 must have been very encouraging for Timothy. He undoubtedly felt very much alone at times there in Ephesus. Paul and his traveling companions had gone to Macedonia across the Aegean Sea. And now

"This Charge I Commit unto Thee."

he had to single-handedly straighten out a dangerous heresy in the church. I'm sure he must have felt defeated more than once. But it is quite possible that this letter came at a time when Timothy needed it most. It reminded him that Paul had not forgotten about him, and that he and the others were praying for him.

The situation in which Timothy found himself is not unlike that of the colorful Old Testament prophet Elijah. The story of his challenge to the 400 prophets of Ba'al is one of the great high points of our Bible story.

In the story Elijah challenges 400 prophets of Ba'al to meet him at the top of Mt. Carmel and prove that their god was more powerful than Yahweh, the God of Israel. The prophets of Ba'al were to erect an altar, place a sacrifice on it, and call on their god to start a fire to consume the sacrifice. They built the altar and began their prayers. Nothing happened. They pleaded louder and louder for Ba'al to hear them. Again, nothing happened. No matter what they did to try to persuade their god to send down fire, there was no response.

Then it was Elijah's turn. He built an altar and put the sacrifice on it. But he was so sure of God's power and faithfulness that before he prayed he drenched the altar with water. Then he prayed. In a moment the fire came and consumed not only the sacrifice, but also the altar and the altar that was erected to Ba'al as well. God had proven that He was God, and that Ba'al had no real power.

Elijah was the victor in the contest. This so enraged the evil queen, Jezebel, that she threatened to kill Elijah within twenty-four hours. In terror he ran south to Beersheba and then on into the Negev where he hid for his life in a cave. There, in a state of fear and deep depression he cried out to God. He complained that he had been very faithful to the Lord, that he was all alone, and that Jezebel was now trying to take his life.

Even as he spoke there came a great howling wind and a thunderstorm. Elijah expected to hear God's voice in the storm, but he did not find Him there. Instead, God answered him, patiently and quietly, in a still small voice. God said to Elijah that there were yet 7,000 people in Israel who had not succumbed to Ba'al worship. His presence was still with Elijah, and the encouragement sent him on his way, renewed in his task.

Neither Elijah nor Timothy was alone in his service for the Lord—and neither are we.

Paul now becomes specific in his instructions to Timothy, "This charge I commit unto thee,"—hold onto the faith and a good conscience (1:18–20). In other words, do not be discouraged; stand firm and let your faith in Christ and your good conscience see you through this heresy-fighting task until it is completed.

Once again we see Paul the great encourager at work. He knew all too well the difficulty of Timothy's assignment. All of us can be a part of this "ministry of encouragement"

The Charge to Timothy.

A view of the paving stones on the Via Egnatia in Philippi. When Paul and Silas and Timothy disembarked at Neapolis from Troas, they traveled the few miles inland to Philippi on this very road.

today simply by writing letters like this one to those we know who have tough jobs to do and who need our encouragement. We all have our moments when we desperately need the affirmation of our fellow Christians. It may be a letter, a telephone call, a quiet word, or an arm around our shoulders that reminds us in a critical moment that we're not alone. As with Elijah, God is always present with us, and there are many other people serving God, too.

Then Paul contrasts Timothy's faithfulness with some who have abandoned their faith—"have made a shipwreck" of their lives (1:19). This was familiar imagery to both of them, for by this time Paul had been through several shipwreck experiences.

Two of those who had given up their faith were Alexander and Hymenaeus. Of them, Paul says, "…whom I had delivered unto Satan, that they may learn not to blaspheme" (1:20). As we learned earlier, the phrase "delivered unto Satan" referred to excommunication from the Church. This seems to have been one of two or three cases of excommunication in the New Testament.

The first incident where instructions called for dismissing someone from the fellowship of believers is found in Matthew 18:15–17. As you reread these three verses you will note the care that was taken to help the offending person to repent of the wrong committed. However, if that person refused to make things right, he was dismissed from the fellowship and treated as an outsider.

The second incident involved the man in Corinth who had an adulterous relationship with his stepmother. In both cases the mood was not angry judgmentalism, but was an attempt to help the offenders learn the truth, repent, and eventually be reconciled to the church.

Now Paul directs his attention to Hymenaeus and Alexander, members of the church in Ephesus. They were "delivered to Satan" in order to learn not to misrepresent the truth of the gospel of Christ by their heretical teaching of "fables and endless genealogies" (1:4). The Hymenaeus mentioned here and in 2 Timothy 2:17 may have been one of the first teachers of the Gnostic heresy discussed earlier in this lesson.

The name Alexander is mentioned three times in relationship to Paul in the New Testament. One is in the book of Acts where a Jew named Alexander tried to speak to the crowd at Ephesus when Paul was arrested there for preaching the gospel. The second Alexander is mentioned in 2 Timothy as a coppersmith who had "done him much evil" (2 Tim. 4:14).

The third Alexander is the one in our present Scripture. He was a Christian disciple who was a teacher in the church at Ephesus. But he had gone astray in his doctrine and had become associated with other false teachers. And Paul was so strongly opposed to their false teaching that he not only excommunicated them from the church, but he also left Timothy in Ephesus to restore order in the church.

In the introductory comments to Timothy in this first chapter, Paul has encouraged him to be strong and stick with his leadership and disciplinary task even though it may be hard. And he has reminded Timothy that he is not alone but is supported by the Lord and upheld by his fellow Christians. That pattern of faithfulness applies equally to us in the twentieth century as it did to Timothy in the first century.

Paul begins now in this second chapter to give specific instructions (exhortations) to Timothy as he assumes leadership in the Ephesian church. As we read and reflect on these instructions, we get a rather vivid picture of just how the early church functioned. Then, I believe, as we reflect on that picture, we can gain remarkable insight into how we as individual Christians and the church as a whole can best serve our world today.

The Apostle first instructs Timothy to teach the importance of prayer, "I exhort therefore, that, *first of all*, supplications, prayers, intercessions, and giving of thanks, be made for *all* men" (2:1, italics mine). These words make it clear that in Paul's mind, praying is of primary importance for the Christian.

We get the impression here from Paul's wording that praying isn't an optional exercise that we go through at a specific time or when we're in the mood. Rather, it is of first importance if we are to be spiritually healthy and effective Christians.

But there's more. Paul is telling Timothy that the Ephesian Christians are to pray for "all men." They were not just to pray for their Christian brothers and sisters in Ephesus—they were to pray for their non-Christian neighbors in Ephesus as well. There's a universality here that is most important for us. We learn from this that we

Paul Begins to Give Instructions.

are not just to pray for our little group...not just for people who understand and interpret the gospel the way we do.

The kind of prayer Paul is writing about here is not a casual religious exercise in which a few especially devout Christians participate while the rest relax around the edges as spectators. Honest and fervent prayer is a dynamic and energizing experience that involves concentration and commitment; it is alive and active.

Betty and Mildred were two retired women who lived in my neighborhood. They were both lovely ladies and delightful to be around. But they couldn't get along with each other. For a time, both of them served on the women's club board. Every meeting was a disaster and ended in an argument between the two of them.

After a time, this standoff began to bother Mildred. Somehow her attitude toward Betty didn't square with her Christian principles, so she went to her minister for advice. His words shocked Mildred: "Have you prayed for Betty? I mean, have you really prayed for her? Have you prayed that her problems will be solved and that she will find comfort and guidance in the midst of the loneliness and confusion she seems to feel? I suspect that if you sincerely do that for one week, something dramatic will happen."

The next day at the end of her prayer time, Mildred added, "And I pray for Betty." Somehow she knew that wasn't the answer, for her pastor had told her to "really pray." So, the next day she tried again. Only this time she really concentrated her thoughts on Betty. From then on, she just couldn't get Betty off her mind.

Finally, one day Mildred called Betty and invited her to lunch. And from that slow and hesitant beginning their friendship grew. Today they are active members of a prayer group. Mildred had learned an important lesson— you just can't pray honestly for somebody and continue to harbor ill feelings toward them! It was this kind of prayer Paul was writing about here.

Pray for Those in Authority. Paul then goes on to include specifically in the "all" they were to pray for, kings and "all that are in authority; that we may lead a quiet and peaceable life in all godliness and honesty" (2:2). During the earliest days of the church it wouldn't have been difficult for Christians to pray for the

Roman authorities that ruled the empire. At that time followers of "the Way" were considered a sect of Judaism and were protected by Roman law. But during the second half of the first century, all of this changed as emperor worship became the law. The Christians, of course, refused to consider anyone Lord but Jesus, and for this "disloyalty" they were subjected to severe persecution. Yet even during such times of stress and pain they were to pray for all in authority because this was God's will and He wanted "all men to be saved, and to come unto the knowledge of the truth" (2:3–4). And the truth Paul reaffirms is "there is one God, and one mediator between God and men, the man Christ Jesus; Who gave himself a ransom for all, to be testified in due time" (2:5–6).

Paul's words in these verses were a dramatic statement of faith. No religion of the time, not even Judaism, believed that people had direct access to God. But the Christian—you and me—has direct access to God through Christ's love and redeeming action. And then Paul goes on to say that the Christian is to pray "lifting up holy hands, without wrath and doubting" (2:8). Here the Apostle points Timothy to an old Jewish picture of people being in God's presence with clean hands and a pure heart as they actively live out the love of God in a real world.

The point is made! Paul believes prayer can change the world. But this doesn't happen by "saying" prayers or "reading" prayers—by spectator praying. We Christians can make a difference in our world by earnest and involved praying for *all* people, including the president, congressmen, governors, and those who direct local government.

Women and the Church.

As we move into these last few verses in our Scripture for this lesson Paul gives Timothy some specific advice on how the Christian women in Ephesus should look and act (2:9–15). We don't know precisely what prompted these particular words of instruction, but it is not unreasonable to assume that there were those who were abusing their newly discovered freedom in Christ.

There have been varying interpretations of these verses throughout all Christian history, but it seems most likely that Paul was addressing himself to a localized problem that prevailed in Ephesus and possibly in the other young churches as well. It will be helpful, though, in our study to be reminded about the status of women in New Testament times.

The Jewish woman of that time had no rights whatsoever. To her father and husband she wasn't much more than a piece of property. In spite of the glowing words of tribute we find in Proverbs 31, Jewish women had no influence outside the home; their duty was to keep house and attend to the comfort of husbands and family. The attitude of Jewish men toward women is well expressed in the morning prayer when men thanked God that they were not gentiles, slaves, or women.

Jewish women were relegated to a lesser area in the synagogue and were to keep quiet. And an especially devout rabbi wouldn't speak to a woman on the street, and this included women in his own family.

Non-Jewish women of the first century were nonpersons as well. The woman's place in Greek religions was virtually nonexistent, except for the temple prostitutes. A wife was the property of her husband. She never ventured out in public alone.

It is against this background that Paul is writing. The Good News of the gospel released women from this kind of bondage, and it is possible that some of them went overboard in their expression of freedom. This accounts, I believe, for Paul's warning that Christian women should dress modestly and not like the pagan temple prostitutes that roamed the streets. He urges them to be involved in doing good things and "to learn in silence." Actually, "learning in silence" is pretty good advice for all of us.

As I wrote earlier, these verses are difficult for us to understand, for we can't be sure just what was on Paul's mind or the problems he was addressing. We do know that under the Apostle's leadership women occupied a prominent place in the early church, even as they did in Jesus' ministry. Throughout the centuries Christianity has given women a revered place in society and in the church.

The important thing for us in our present study is to remember all of Paul's words about women as they're found throughout all of his writings. To do this is to avoid the rigidity that has at times plagued society. It is this spirit that prompted Matthew Henry, the eighteenth-century commentary writer, to say that woman was "not made out of his [man's] head to rule over him, nor out of his feet to be trampled upon by him, but out of his side to be equal with him, under his arm to be protected, and near his heart to be beloved."

Our Scripture lesson closes with a comment by Paul that Bible teachers have struggled with over the centuries, "...she shall be saved in childbearing" (2:15). Some have seen this as a reference to the birth of Jesus by Mary. Others have interpreted this as referring to motherhood in general, and still others have related it to the messianic message that seems to come through in Genesis 3:15. We may have to be satisfied with the idea that this is one of the very few instances where we can't be entirely sure of Paul's meaning.

A Summation.

As we reflect on these thirty-five verses at the beginning of Paul's letter to Timothy, we discover sound teaching both for the Ephesian Christians in their first-century setting and for us in the closing years of the twentieth century. As Christians, we are to live lives that are consistent with the teachings of Jesus. We are to pray for "all" men, including those who hold positions of authority. And we are to "listen" and study to be authentic witnesses—ministers—to the Good News wherever we live.

Lord, Let prayer be more and more a part of my life. Make me a person who takes time and prays. AMEN.

WHAT THIS SCRIPTURE MEANS TO ME—1 Timothy 1–2

How my mother did it, I will never know. She fried chicken, baked biscuits, and boiled every bit of our hot water over a wood-burning stove. She did this on hot summer days when the Texas temperature soared over the hundred mark. And in the chill of winter we rushed the water from the stove to the bathtub and scrubbed quickly before the water got cold.

In those Depression days of the 1930s, I rode two and a half miles to school behind my father on a nice old bay horse named Bess. It was fun at times, but it got tiresome day in and day out and was downright unpleasant in rain or freezing weather.

Rarely do I see water, hot and plentiful, gushing into the sink or out of the shower, that I don't feel a warm sense of gratitude. All that hot water without building a fire!

Slipping under the wheel of a comfortable car, air conditioned in summer and heated in winter, makes me feel like a queen, light-years away from the four-legged transportation of my childhood. But there is just no way I can forget where I came from or how life was in those early days, even though things are drastically different now. From time to time I feel impelled to say something about these very ordinary, everyday blessings that we so readily take for granted now.

Paul had apparently a similar impulse, in the first chapter of 1 Timothy, when he wrote to "my own son in the faith" and gave him some very practical advice for dealing with the problems in the church at Ephesus. Then in verses 12 and 13, in almost the next breath after his words about murderers and liars, Paul remembered who *he* was and what *he* did before the glorious grace of our Lord changed his life. Then he stopped to recall his past ignorance and unbelief, persecution and blasphemy, and with words like love and faith, forgiveness and overflowing grace, crescendoed in his praise of a loving Lord into a fantastic doxology of joy.

These verses are thrilling to me as I reflect on them. I am a sinner, too, but forgiven! I formerly insulted my Lord with ignorance and disbelief, but grace overflows for me, too. I received mercy, and Paul puts into words feelings I try to express but cannot. With the reading of this Scripture I am swept along with him to shout the heretofore inexpressible: "Now unto the King eternal, immortal, invisible, the only wise God, be honour and glory for ever and ever. Amen" (1 Tim. 1:17).

Exciting as the doxology is, in the very next verse, it is right back to the "real world" for Timothy. And this causes me to remember that even in my high moments the world is out there for me, too. I know life can't be all "hallelujah." Paul's doxology, squeezed in between dealing with faithless teachers and the results of a shipwrecked faith certainly give me perspective through both my ups and downs.

I remember so well one of those freezing winter days of my childhood. My mother was in Bess' saddle on the ride to school with me, half holding on in the "rumble-seat," as we began to cross a bridge not far from our house. When Bess' hooves hit the ice on that bridge, her back feet slid in under her front feet. Mom jumped off, luckily, and I simply slid off right onto the concrete, catapulting, bullet-like, backward about ten feet.

The frightened horse floundered, regained her footing, and then trotted off through a neighbor's pasture. We then gathered up scattered books and lunches, quite sure there wouldn't be any school that day for me, but in just a few minutes we saw our neighbor coming toward us with the horse in tow.

The spill on the bridge had certainly made the usually uneventful trip to school different and exciting. It was still cold when we got back on the horse, and there were still two more miles to go to get to school, but we were safe and well, relieved and happy, and on our way again.

Through the years the memory of that experience has been a small reminder that ordinary days with their "spills"—their ups and downs—also have sudden and unexpected moments of joy. Grace abounds as we live in the world.

LESSON 2
1 TIMOTHY 3—4

Leadership in the Church

Dear Lord, In my leading, help me to be always led by You. Help me to not rush ahead of You, or to lag, resistantly, behind. Let me be in step with Your Spirit, ever listening for Your still, small voice. AMEN.

In the second chapter of Acts, Luke graphically describes the scene which is commonly accepted as the birth of the Christian Church. In line with Jesus' instructions the apostles met together in prayer. Then on "the day of Pentecost...suddenly there came a sound from heaven as of a rushing mighty wind, and it filled all the house where they were sitting. And there appeared unto them cloven tongues like as of fire, and it sat upon each of them. And they were all filled with the Holy Ghost..." (Acts 2:2–3).

Why Leaders Were Needed.   When the apostles had received the Holy Spirit, we are then told that they went out into the city of Jerusalem and began immediately to preach the Good News of Jesus Christ. At the conclusion of Peter's magnificent sermon that day, Luke writes, "Then they that gladly received his word were baptized: and the same day there were added unto them about three thousand souls" (Acts 2:41).

The results of their continued witnessing were electrifying as Luke adds, "And the Lord added to the church daily such as should be saved." The Christian community grew and spread like an out of control fire in a dry forest.

During the church's earliest days, the apostles were the leaders. But soon three things happened that called for a change in leadership roles. First, the church became too large for the apostles to handle alone. There was just no way they could direct all activities. So, as a first step deacons were appointed who were responsible primarily for the charitable ministries.

Second, not long after Pentecost and the martyrdom of Stephen, the persecution of Christians under the leadership of Saul of Tarsus became intense. And it was at this time that Jewish Christians fled from Jerusalem and Judea to the outlying regions of Palestine and even into Syria. And since the apostles for the most part remained close to Jerusalem to oversee the churches there, these outlying churches needed leadership.

Third, the Christian flame soon spread more and more into gentile territory—into Syria and what was then known as Asia Minor (modern Turkey). People were converted from Greek and Roman paganism and needed guidance and direction in their newfound faith. Early confusion developed because of the odd mixture of the Greek and Roman religions and Judaism and Christianity.

All of this called for a careful selection of regional and local leadership as a means of insuring the purity of the church's teaching.

Church Leaders.

Paul, of course, was very sensitive to the importance of proper local church leadership. And so in writing now to Timothy about the need for leadership in the Ephesian churches Paul lays down some guidelines to be followed in selecting those leaders. Two specific leadership types are mentioned in the early part of our Scripture lesson (3:1–13).

Paul's first reference is to "a bishop"—*episkopos* (3:1). The Greek word actually means "overseer" or "superintendent." Later translations reflect this usage. The bishop was a local leader who was selected to preside at church gatherings, the celebration of the Lord's Supper, and baptisms. He also represented the local congregation at regional meetings. The word bishop as it is used here is quite different from our understanding of it today. There weren't then the ecclesiastical associations with the term, and most certainly Paul's purpose here was not to spell out any elaborate form of church organization.

Closely associated with the term "bishop" in the New Testament is another word—*presbuteros*—that also denotes a leader in the church and the Greek word is translated as "elder." This was an old and honorable position in Judaism, and we read where Paul and Barnabas appointed elders in every church (Acts 14:23). And in Titus 1:5 we find Paul instructing Titus to appoint elders in Crete.

There is ample indication in Scripture that at times the two words—bishop and elder—may have been used interchangeably. Then, too, there may have been instances when a chief elder or bishop was selected to be spokesman for the rest at councils and conferences. But the important thing was that these leaders were essential to the spiritual holiness of the church. This is why it was necessary to exercise extreme care in their selection.

Qualifications for Leadership.

Paul now sets down sixteen attributes of a good overseer or superintendent (3:2–7), but first he insists that anyone aspiring to be an overseer-leader must want above all else to do a good and noble work—he or she must feel especially "called." No one, neither a clergyperson nor a layperson, should ever assume the leadership role in a church because of the honor and prestige involved or because someone else expects it. Rather, the bishop, the overseer, the pastor assumes his or her role of responsibility because of a "call" from God and an impelling desire to do "good work."

Next, I should add that being a good overseer or leader *does* take hard work! Bishops, superintendents, pastors, as they seek to lead a congregation, direct spiritual growth, and minister to the personal needs of people, must be committed to hard and grueling work that demands the giving of time and energy. I once heard of a particular church leader who introduced himself this way, "I am the Presiding Bishop of the Episcopal Church. I have a widow and two children." Paul knew all about that kind of selfless giving of time and energy in his compulsion to get the Good News of hope in Christ to as many people as he possibly could.

We'll not attempt to examine all sixteen of the attributes of a good overseer-leader that Paul lists here, but we will

A view of the Amphitheater in Philippi. It is not unlikely that this was a familiar site to Timothy whose name was most familiar to the Christians in Philippi. Timothy shared in the greetings that opened Paul's letter to the Philippians.

look at certain of these in some detail. It will be helpful as we study them to remember that even though Paul is writing about the leadership qualities of a bishop or overseer, these characteristics actually apply to any of us who assume a position of responsibility in the church.

First, Paul writes that a leader (bishop) "must be blameless" (3:2)—above reproach, above question. He or she must be "vigilant, sober, of good behaviour, given to hospitality." In other words, our actions are to square with the faith we profess. Furthermore, our reputation is to be impeccable not only with fellow Christians, but with those "which are without" (3:7)—non-Christians in our neighborhoods and towns. To be an effective leader and witness to the Good News of Jesus Christ our name and reputation must be trustworthy. The wisdom writer put it this way, "A good name is rather to be chosen than great riches, and loving favor rather than silver and gold" (Prov. 22:1).

Packed into this same verse in 1 Timothy is another attribute of leadership in the church—the ability to teach. It is through teaching that we develop and mature in our faith. In our New Testament we learn that teaching is one of the gifts of the Spirit and is given for the building up of the church. But I believe that each of us in our own way is to be an affirmer and teacher. We are to study and apply ourselves so we can properly interpret God's truth in words and actions to our fellow Christians (2 Tim. 2:15). We are to be participants and not merely spectators in the Christian walk.

Now, since I've spent so much time, and rightly so, on Chapter 3:2, I should say that we don't know for certain exactly what Paul meant by his comment that a bishop should be "the husband of one wife." There are two or three possible meanings that have been given for this statement, but since Paul did not make a precise application here of what he meant, I shall not attempt to. We can be certain, though, that he had a specific reason at that time for insisting that an overseer should be married—the husband of one wife.

There is another characteristic of leadership that Paul mentions that I want to underline here, "Not a novice, lest being lifted up with pride he fall into the condemnation of the devil" (3:6).

The Apostle seems to be suggesting that we not heap leadership responsibilities on new Christians before they have the experience and maturity to handle either the pressure or the power. It is tremendously important that we not push someone into a position of prominence or leadership in the church before he or she is ready.

We've all seen examples, I'm sure, of athletes or actors or songwriters or politicians—celebrity types—who are set up on pedestals and become instant authorities right after their conversion. Paul's instruction here is very practical for us in our late twentieth-century churches. We are to nurture and build up young Christians and not press them beyond their capabilities.

Then in his super-practical way Paul writes about a leadership quality that has important implications for every Christian. He writes that a bishop is "One that ruleth well his own house" (3:4–5). In other words, all of the important characteristics that a leader displays around the church are to be a part of home and family life. We are to be responsible and loving leaders at home as well as at church, and we are to live out our Christian faith among those who know us best—our families.

We've all heard the horror stories about leaders who spent all of their time "in the service of the Lord," but neglected their own home and families. I believe Paul is telling Timothy—and us—that the responsible leader is not to neglect home and family.

Household Management—an Important Quality in Leadership.

Before leaving our brief discussion of the attributes or characteristics of an overseer-leader, I want to refer to three descriptive words in verse 2, "given to hospitality." If this characteristic was important in the first-century church, I have to feel it is many times more important in our bustling and impersonal urban society today.

Feeling alone even on a crowded street is all too common today. Deep and true friendships are difficult to sustain in our society. And yet we all long for others to "take us in" to their hearts and homes. At the same time, though, we are all guilty of becoming so involved with the routines of our own lives that we tend to regard people as interruptions instead of opportunities for fellowship and spiritual growth.

But in this very brief reminder Paul gives us what may be one of the most important attributes of a church leader today—be friendly, be open, be warm and hospitable in our service for the Lord. Take time to be an affirming friend to your fellow Christians.

Hospitable and Friendly.

As we can see, Paul set very high standards for leaders in the early church. And he continues now to give Timothy a list of attributes for deacons—another form of early church leadership (3:8–13).

You may recall from our studies in Acts that the first deacons were selected to help the apostles carry out cer-

Deacons: Their Function and Responsibilities.

tain functions of ministry—they were to care for the physical needs of any of their group who were in need (Acts 6). And so Paul now turns his attention to the qualifications for those who serve the Lord and the church in this role.

As we look at the characteristics of deacons, we shouldn't be surprised that they're not much different from those of bishop-overseer-leaders. They were to be trustworthy—"proved"—and their values were to be in line with the teachings of Jesus. Deacons were to be respected members of home and community—moderate and circumspect in their personal habits and lives.

Then we find a wealth of meaning in Paul's statement in verse 9 when he writes that deacons should hold "the mystery of the faith in a pure conscience." Although the love and grace of God is a mystery and beyond our ability to understand, we are all as Christians and leaders to accept that grace and then in turn share it with others in "great boldness in the faith which is in Christ Jesus" (3:13).

Again, we see the practicality in Paul's words here, as we reflect on the attributes for church leadership the Apostle was giving Timothy. They have a very up-to-date sound and in fact apply to all of us as we witness through words and actions to our faith. Even those (deacons) who were not pastor-leaders were active witnesses to the Good News.

We are all under the same kind of compulsion as Peter and John in the New Testament story. When they were arrested in Jerusalem, their witness was simple and yet profound, "For we cannot but speak the things we have seen and heard" (Acts 4:20). And we find it was this same compulsion that caused two early deacons—Stephen and Phillip—to move out boldly in their witnessing (Acts 7, 8).

A Personal Note.   Paul next interrupts his instructions to Timothy with a personal note (3:14–16). Here the Apostle expresses the hope that he can visit Ephesus soon, however, he knows he may be delayed. I get the feeling here that Paul is doing two things. First, he is letting Timothy know that he has confidence in him.

This kind of affirmation is extremely important. I recall so well one time when I was serving as an associate in a church and was scheduled to attend an important luncheon with my senior minister. On the day of the luncheon he was unable to attend, but when I saw him he said, "I really wasn't worried. I knew you would handle everything well." That vote of confidence gave me great assurance.

Second, I believe that Paul was reaffirming his belief as to how Christians should conduct themselves in the work of the church, the household and family of God.

And then Paul ends this personal note with another of his brief but majestic descriptions of the nature of Christ (3:16). This may well have been an excerpt from one of the early hymns of the church or a fragment of a creedal statement. Here we confront the great "mystery of godliness":

> God was seen in the flesh,
> He was affirmed by the Holy Spirit,
> He was seen by angels,
> He was preached to the gentiles,
> He was believed on in the world,
> He returned to His Father in glory.

Problems in "the Latter Times."

Next, we see Paul moving on in his letter to Timothy to a discussion of the heresy that was plaguing the church at Ephesus (4:1–5). In doing so, though, he used a phrase that tells us a lot about Paul's attitude and life, yet it is one we often misunderstand. I am referring to his words, "the latter times."

From the moment of his conversion, Paul believed that he was living in the "latter days." God had spoken finally in Jesus Christ. The Holy Spirit had come. And all that remained was for Christ to return to claim His new society, His kingdom. Whether that event occurred the next day or in a thousand years, the task was the same: to spread throughout the world the Good News of God's grace.

Paul's whole life-style expressed this conviction. He never looked back and was always in a hurry to do the things that he felt were important. He was driven to move on to the next town, the next synagogue, the best place to witness to the gentiles about the Good News of Jesus Christ. For him, there wasn't time to get involved with "the things of the world." He didn't believe in making permanent attachments to earthly responsibilities, and he felt strongly that a preoccupation with details in this present life kept a person from concentrating on "heavenly things."

Paul practiced what he preached, and he encouraged others to do the same. Yet it finally occurred to him that everyone didn't have the same call he did. For those who did continue in a "normal" life-style, he insisted that all things be done sincerely, purely, and in a manner consistent with the best customs (see 1 Cor. 7 & 11).

Finally, Paul's writings also revealed his belief that he was living in the "latter days." In one place, he speaks in this imagery: "The night is far spent, the day is at hand: let us therefore cast off the works of darkness, and let us put on the whole armor of light" (Rom. 13:12). In another letter he speaks of the day of the Lord "coming as a thief in the night" (1 Thess. 5:2).

From his vantage point Paul *was* living in the last days. As he saw it, everyone who lived after the time of Christ was in the last days. And because of this there were certain events that could be expected to happen. Among those events were the advent of false teachers and false doctrines in the Church. But it would be a mistake to interpret those events as proof that the end of time as we know it was just around the corner. Many faithful and well-intentioned Christians have done that throughout history and have been sorely disappointed and even disillusioned.

The Heresy in the Ephesian Church.

Now, let us look once more at the Gnosticism that Paul attacked at Ephesus. In the first verses of Chapter 4, he again recognizes that these false teachers have departed from the faith of Christ that had been introduced to them by Paul and the other apostles—having been deceived by "seducing spirits and doctrines of devils" (4:1). You remember they taught among other things that the physical body, and in fact all of matter, was evil. And they then imposed strict rules on their converts that reinforced this false teaching.

Two of these rules that Paul mentions here were the forbidding of marriage and the eating of meat. Now, in making rules like these the Gnostic troublemakers were undermining two of the most basic of human needs—food and procreation. Meat and marriage were forbidden by the heretical ascetics because of their belief that matter and the body were evil.

These kinds of self-mortification were diametrically opposed to God's will and purpose. To teach that physical matter and the human body are evil is to slander God's own creation. Such a false interpretation of God's intention for the human race is utterly contrary to some of the

Bible's earliest instruction. First, after God had completed His creative process, the writer of Genesis 1 wrote, "And God saw every thing that he had made, and, behold, *it was very good*" (1:31, italics mine). And earlier the Genesis writer said, "…and God said unto them, Be fruitful, and multiply, and replenish the earth." And as for food, we have God's word to Noah after the flood, "Every moving thing that liveth shall be meat for you…" (Gen. 9:3).

And so Paul firmly declares that everything God created is good. One of God's greatest gifts is our sexuality—and another is His gift of food, our daily bread. Futhermore, he goes on to say that we are to receive these gifts with thanksgiving (4:3). Indeed, one of the marks of our giving up the faith—of our apostasy—is the rejection and mis-use of the marvelous gifts God has made available to us.

Our mission as Christians in the twentieth century is to be good stewards of the awesome gifts that God has given us—the gifts of life, marriage, family, vocation, of the potential of all modern technology. These are gifts to be used and experienced to the glory of God!

All of life's needs are sanctified for our use by the creative word of God and by our prayers of thanksgiving. And in using them wisely, we, with Timothy and the Ephesian Christians, will be worthy ministers of Jesus Christ, being truly nourished by "the words of faith and of good doctrine" (4:6).

Important Words of Advice.

Paul now moves along with some very practical advice to Timothy about his own personal life and service (4:6–11). And I should add that what we find here is good advice for everyone in all time who is in any way a leader, or even a follower, in the church.

You will remember the setting. Paul has assigned Timothy to the church at Ephesus with specific instructions to correct the errors and false teaching there. This is an enormous task for a young man with little experience. Consequently, Paul now stresses the fact that the difficulties in the church can be corrected by Godly living and good teaching. Good teaching is still the best antidote for error in our Christian walk. Bible study, like we're doing together here, points the way to a mature understanding of our faith. This is our nourishment for life in Christ. "Words of faith and of good doctrine" are to guide us daily in our pilgrimage of faith.

Then Paul picks up on the athletic theme—one near and dear to Ephesians and Greeks. By no means is Paul downgrading physical fitness here (4:8), but he is rather emphasizing the importance of spiritual exercise—of being fit spiritually, of being trained in our Christian faith.

Be an Example.

Always the sensitive and affirmative mentor, Paul realizes the need to assure Timothy that his age need not stand in the way of success, "Let no man despise thy youth" (4:12). It wasn't his age but his character that counted. His instructions were clear, "…be thou an example of the believers, in word, in conversation, in charity, in spirit, in faith, in purity" (4:12).

It wasn't seniority that would get the job done in the church. Rather, Timothy was to live out Christlike love in the ordinariness of life. His thoughts, his conversation, his spirit were all to be directed by the Holy Spirit. This, too, is the final test for us as we work in the church and represent Christ in our neighborhoods and towns. Yes, we are to witness verbally to God's saving goodness, but the true test comes as people hear our conversation and feel our attitudes and spirit. It is our example that speaks louder than anything we can say.

The Use of Gifts.

Paul continues his advice to Timothy by urging him not to neglect "the gift that is in thee" (4:14). When Timothy had been appointed and ordained as a leader in the church, it was recognized that he had certain gifts from God that would be important to his service.

Paul's reminder to Timothy not to neglect his gifts may well have been just that—a reminder. This comment might also have been initiated by Paul's exceptional insight. He was very familiar with the highs and lows that characterize our Christian walk. He knew how easy it is to get bogged down in the day-to-day struggles and frustrations and details to the neglect of the most important things—the use of our special God-given gifts. It is often terribly easy to miss the best by being distracted with the good.

It is very possible Paul's advice here to his young friend was not to get too busy just being busy and neglect what was most important—exercising the unique gifts that were his. I've known writers that get so busy sharpening pencils, filing papers, emptying wastebaskets, and cleaning the desk they never have time to write. Such a waste of gifts is a tragedy in the work of the church.

Each of us—ministers and lay persons—have been given special abilities and talents—gifts. There are things you and I can do in service for our church and community that are peculiar to our particular abilities. Paul's advice not to neglect those gifts is as important in your town and mine as it was to Timothy in ancient Ephesus.

Paul closes out this part of our lesson by urging his young friend to meditate and reflect on all that he has read so far (4:15–16). He tells Timothy that much of his personal growth will emerge from his private reflections on his life and ministry and on the doctrines of the Christian faith. Paul's idea of meditation and reflection can be a healthy exercise for all of us, for in meditation we listen for the voice of God.

We live in a world where the motion of life pushes us along at breakneck speed. We don't take time to think or reflect, to be in creative communion with God, and so the world molds us instead of our molding the world. We tend to drift along with the crowd, and instead of being originals, we become carbon copies of everyone around us.

But each of us has a unique place in God's kingdom—His realm in our world. It is as we meditate and reflect daily on our personal relationship with God and our Christian faith and teachings that we are molded into the kind of people He wants us to be. This is spiritual growth; this is becoming "conformed to the image of his Son" (Rom. 8:29).

Paul longs for Timothy to experience this growth and to be an example for everyone to see. Then, Paul tells him, "Thou shalt both save thyself, *and them that hear thee*" (4:16, italics mine).

Meditation and Reflection.

There is no way we can fit ourselves into Timothy's shoes as he reads this letter. He probably knew better than anyone else just how much he needed Paul's confidence and words of advice and encouragement. In a way, I think I can identify with how he probably felt because of my own experience with my first assignment as assistant in the recreation department of my home church.

My immediate responsibilities involved keeping the recreation areas clean, open, and running smoothly dur-

A Personal Reflection.

ing the afternoons after school and on weekends. It seemed to me then that I had the most important job in the world. But I also knew I needed all the help and advice I could get, and so I leaned heavily on my supervisor.

John became for me what I suspect Paul was for Timothy—not only my supervisor, but my friend and confidant, my big brother and sometimes even a father. For two years he was my teacher, and I was always careful to watch closely everything he did.

I went with John to important meetings, to church functions, to classes, and on personal errands and trips. I learned by watching what he did as well as by listening to

Two views of ruins in Philippi. Because of its strategic location near the Macedonian seaport city of Neapolis and on the heavily traveled Egnatian Way, it is not surprising that Timothy most likely visited here frequently. Timothy's name was evidently quite familiar to the Philippian Christians.

what he said. Time and time again when we were performing some task or working on a problem, he would say, "You won't learn this at seminary." He was right; I didn't. And as I reflect back now over those years I see that most of what I do in the ministry I learned from John. His words of instruction, correction, and encouragement were the most important part of my education and growth as a Christian minister.

What a marvelous opportunity we all have to be a Paul to a Timothy or a John to a Jim. I think being a friend, a mentor, an encourager to a fellow Christian may be one of our best service opportunities for the Lord and His church. At the same time, though, such an opportunity carries a heavy responsibility. It is indeed sobering to know there may be people watching us right now and interpreting what we say and do as being the Christian way.

This lesson speaks very pointedly to each of us. Being a Christian and a Christian leader of any kind calls for us to

be a certain kind of people—a people of the Way, committed to put into daily practice the teachings of Jesus. We are to *do* the Good News. Then we are to *be* authentic witnesses to those around us of life *in Christ*. Furthermore, we are to be sensitive in our use of the particular gifts God has given us and assume the responsibility for being helpers and encouragers, as well as models, to those around us who need and want our friendship and guidance.

An impossible task? Not really if we thoughtfully reflect and act on Paul's closing words of advice to young Timothy in this lesson—we are to carefully guard the quality of our own life and teaching and make certain our words and actions are motivated by the love of Christ and His Spirit. It is then, and then only, that we can become a Paul to our Timothys.

Father God, Let me make time to meditate and reflect on You, our relationship, Your Word, Your plans for my life. Lord, help me not to be a victim of the urgent, but to give You control of the time You've graciously given me. AMEN.

WHAT THIS SCRIPTURE MEANS TO ME—1 Timothy 3—4

When I read "For bodily exercise profiteth little..."(1 Tim. 4:8), I thought, "Hurray, I don't have to walk my mile today. And I sure hope Paul meant that jogging was a sin so I don't have to feel inferior to those slim, lithe people who pass me without even breathing hard."

If I'm honest, though, I know that is *not* what the Scripture means, but it does grab my attention in our exercise-conscious world. The important phrase, however, is earlier in the verse, where Paul urges Timothy to "exercise thyself rather unto godliness; for while bodily training is of some value, godliness is of value in every way" (RSV).

Does Paul mean that we should train as vigorously as a varsity football player does during the long, hot days of August in preparation for the October game? Could he possibly be saying that we should be as disciplined and work as hard in our Christian training as an athlete who is preparing for the Olympic Games?

Our younger daughter had watched her older sister work her way up from the elementary first spot on the recital program to a higher place that indicated she was beginning to learn to play the piano. After one student program when Polly had played exceptionally well, her teacher asked little Chris, "Are you going to take piano lessons someday?"

"No," replied the six-year-old, "I don't know any pieces to play at the recital."

That was her impression after having heard her sister practice hours and hours. Nobody in our house could have helped but hear those practice sessions! We *all* knew every note of "Lively Lil' Lizard," "Fleecy Clouds," and "Tick, Tock, the Clock Shop." Chris was there when we had to *make* Polly practice, but somehow all of that training seemed unimportant to her. She thought you had to know the piece before you learned to play.

Of course, that kind of thinking sounds strange to an adult, but just think how frustrated we feel when we don't immediately become the kind of Christians we know we should be. We're inclined to kick and scream or give up when we fail. But training in godliness is essential, too. We can be moved emotionally to praise, to pray, to worship, but much of the time, being Christian in our actions is a matter of discipline.

I can look at myself in the mirror and say, "Katy, you can choose to be godly in your response to Jane's untrue and cutting remark. Or you can choose to throw out the window what you *know* to be a believer's reactions and make a big, bad scene."

Then as I have continued to think about Paul's words, "...exercise thyself...unto godliness," I've decided to type them on a card and paste it to the dashboard of my car. I am sorely in need of exercising godliness out in traffic when a zippy little car darts unexpectedly into my lane, scaring the daylights out of me. At such moments I'm appalled at the feelings of hostility that surge through my mind and displace any thoughts of love that should be there.

So I read Paul's words again, "Meditate upon these things; give thyself wholly to them; that thy profiting may appear to all. Take heed unto thyself..." I will—I must—be aware of the times that I am most likely to react negatively, and *train* myself in godliness. I must *practice* the presence of the living Lord in those shadowy places.

As our daughters neared the age when they would start dating, we began to play a game in the car while on errands or on the way to church. I would pretend to be a boy who was taking them out for the first time and make outrageous suggestions of things to do. And they would make equally outlandish and funny responses.

But then we would eventually get around to talking about the real value system they wanted in boy-girl relationships. We "trained" them so they would be prepared to act in social situations as they felt young Christians should.

Paul's instructions here to Timothy about our behavior as Christians are extremely important. How important? Read again what he says, "...continue in them: for in doing this thou shalt both save thyself, and them that hear thee."

LESSON 3
1 TIMOTHY 5–6

Relationships in the Church

Lord God, Let my relationships with believers in Your church be a sweet smelling offering to You. Lord, help me to overlook offenses, to be sensitive toward the feelings of others and not just my own, to look for ways to serve others—that You might be blessed. Amen.

In our last lesson we left Paul giving Timothy advice about his own personal life and spiritual development. Now, the Apostle moves on to advise his young friend on the proper way for him to handle and work with individual members in the congregation. Then he singles out two specific groups that he feels deserve special attention: widows and elders.

Paul first advises Timothy to "Rebuke not an elder" (5:1). The term "elder" as it is used here refers to the older men in the congregation. The older men should not be rebuked in an antagonistic manner, but should be "entreated" and reasoned with in the same kind of respectful manner that a person would use with his or her own father.

Most of us can identify, I am sure, with Paul's advice here as we think of our own fathers. Sometimes our reasoned argument, approached with respect, would change

Older Men Should Be Treated As Fathers.

53

his mind. Sometimes it would not. But an antagonistic challenge to his authority *never* worked.

I experienced several of both kinds of confrontation with my father when I was a teenager. Looking back now I wonder why I didn't learn at the time that I had a 50/50 chance of changing his mind if I approached him respectfully. But I had no chance if I told him that he didn't know what was going on in the real world, that he was old-fashioned, and that I was the only person in my high school whose father wasn't agreeable.

A story about my early days of driving may illustrate my point. I was legally allowed to drive in my home state when I was fifteen years old. I remember reading in the Drivers' License Examination booklet that "driving a motor vehicle in this state is a privilege granted by the State of Louisiana." But in my youthful "wisdom" I believed that driving was the inalienable right granted to everyone.

When I got my license, I was ready to take up residence in the car. I think I could have driven 24 hours a day. My dad didn't agree with me, though, and since he had the keys, his was the prevailing opinion. I argued till I was hoarse that everyone my age drove to school, and that rear tires always wore out before the front ones did.

Finally, I asked him if I could take him driving with me. I showed him that I was a competent driver, that I was safe and considerate, and I told him that if I wore out another set of tires too soon, I would buy the new ones. It worked! From that moment on, Dad seemed to stop worrying about my driving, and he let me go just about anywhere I wanted to. Furthermore, he told me I didn't have to buy tires—I could buy gas instead.

Obviously, the approach that recognized my father's authority over the car, and respected that authority, was the proper one. Paul recognized this important truth in relationships and encounters in the church. And so he told Timothy that it was recognition, respect, and compassion that would make for good and smooth relationships in the church.

The older men in the congregation were to be treated like fathers. Timothy and all of his young associates were to show deference and respect for all of the older men. This would also open the way for Timothy to take advantage of the wisdom and counsel of men whose experience in relationships and life could be most helpful. The enthusiasm and exuberance of youth mingled with the experience and understanding of older people makes an unbeatable combination.

Paul then in these opening words also advises Timothy to treat the younger men—his contemporaries—like brothers. And in verse 2 the Apostle continues the family analogy by saying that the older Christian women should be treated like mothers and the younger ones like sisters— "with all purity." Paul spoke volumes in these last three words —Timothy was to conduct himself with the young women in his congregation in a chaste and modest manner.

Paul next directs his attention to a particular group in the church, "Honour widows that are widows indeed" (5:3). The Apostle's instruction here to Timothy and to the church congregation is direct, simple, and compassionate, and it follows in the rich tradition of the Jewish faith.

Widows in the Church.

Nothing could be more expressive of the Christian ideal of love and charity than for the church to assume the responsibility for the well-being of women who had lost their husbands and were alone. In the very beginning, the first-century church took steps to insure that widows and others in need were cared for out of the resources and gifts of their fellow Christians. In fact, as you will remember, the first deacons were appointed to oversee this part of the church's ministry (Acts 6).

The fact that Paul in this part of his letter devotes as much space as he does (5:2–16) to the church's care and oversight of the widows in the congregation seems to speak of a particular problem that was present at that time; however, I believe the implications of the Apostle's instruction are broad and extend even to our responsibilities today.

In the first century there weren't the governmental and charitable agencies in place that we have today. Also it was not possible for women who were left alone through the death of their husbands to earn their own living. So, without outside help these women had no means of staving off the ravages of poverty.

Paul makes it clear in verse 4, though, that the first responsibility for caring for widows in need rested on their families—their children and grandchildren. And the Apostle takes this opportunity to remind them that providing for their mothers and grandmothers in need enables them in a way to repay them for their love and care. But then

Paul goes a step further when he refers to the assuming of this responsibility as being more than just a family duty but a spiritual one as well, "...for that is good and acceptable before God."

It was the accepted norm in Jewish culture to care for one's family, even the extended family. And Paul insists that this was also an essential quality of the Christian faith. In fact, his language is quite strong in verse 8, "But if any provide not for his own, and specially for those of his own house, he hath denied the faith, and is worse than an infidel."

"Widows Indeed."

We have seen in all of our studies just how careful Paul is in his use of language. He is always economical and specific in his selection of words. Such being the case, when he writes that the church is to honor those widows who are "widows indeed," we know that he was undoubtedly choosing his words carefully. It would appear that there were some women in the congregation who were taking advantage of the church's ministry to widows.

And so in verses 9 and 10 Pauls spells out the several qualifications of those who are "widows indeed" and who are to be taken care of by the church if they have need. In addition to trusting God and being prayerful (5:5), they were to have been "the wife of one man," to have had a good reputation, to have set a good example for everyone, to have served in humility and with compassion, to have been faithful in the raising of their children, to have been hospitable, and to have been diligent in their own spiritual growth.

You will notice in verse 9 the reference to widows that are sixty years old. It doesn't seem likely, based on the spirit of these verses, that assistance would be withheld from a widow in need merely because she wasn't sixty years old. And so it has been suggested by some teachers that among the widows there were those who were set aside for a special ministry of prayer and intercession. It was these women who were at least sixty years old, who because of their years of experience were especially suited for this special service.

Widows Who Were Not the Responsibility of the Church.

Paul also makes it clear in his discussion that there were some widows who were not the church's responsibility. First, there were those who had been well provided for by their husbands before death. Then, as we've already discussed, there were those who were provided for by their families.

Next, beginning with verse 11 Paul refers to "younger widows." It would appear that for a widow to qualify for help from the church she had to make a pledge not to re-marry but to spend her time in serving the congregation. Such being the case, young women who had lost their husbands shouldn't take the vow not to marry again be-cause of their very natural physical needs and desires.

Rather, Paul encourages these younger widows to re-marry. He knew they shouldn't be expected to set aside their normal feelings and emotions. But it was important that he clarify this matter here because apparently some of the younger widows in the congregation had vowed to remain single after their husband's death, and then when their grieving period was over, they found it impossible to keep the vow they had made.

The point Paul wants Timothy to understand now is that it is perfectly all right for a young widow to remarry, and it is much better for her not to make a vow than to make it and break it. In other words, based on the custom of the time, if a young woman lost her husband in death, she should conduct her affairs in some proper way so as not to commit herself to serve the church and not marry again.

Then in verse 13 Paul addresses another problem that had apparently arisen in Ephesus. Evidently, some of the young widows being cared for by the congregation had fallen into the lax habit of not applying themselves dili-gently to the work of the church but had become "tattlers …and busybodies, speaking things which they ought not." And so he suggests they would be better off to remar-ry and assume family responsibilities. In addition to the joy and satisfaction this would bring, they wouldn't have time to be gossiping busybodies.

And finally, Paul says once again that each person should be diligent to care for any widows in the family so as not to burden the church unnecessarily (5:16).

A Twentieth-Century Application.

It is true as I've already explained that Paul's words here about the care of widows was related to a specific problem in the first-century church. And on the surface these verses don't seem to have much, if any, relationship to us and to our churches today. But it would be a mistake, I believe, to miss the richness of Paul's teaching here by applying it only to that first-century problem.

Our mission as twentieth-century Christians is to care for and about each other. First-century Christians were recognized as such by their neighbors by the way they loved each other. And that love was not characterized by static feelings, but by energized and acted-out emotions. Their love and concern for each other wasn't a Sunday affair. Rather, it colored all of their relationships throughout every day of the week.

Then, in addition to caring for each other, we are to take a page out of Jesus' book and have a deep, caring concern for our neighbors and people across the world who are *not* Christians. Jesus didn't only feed the hungry and heal the sick who were "Jews like Him." Instead, He responded to human need and anguish wherever He found it. This is our model for today! Our responsibility to the hungry, the displaced, and the sick, reaches from New York's Bowery to Los Angeles' Main Street, to Uganda to Cambodia to Central America to Ethiopia to Afghanistan—anywhere there is need. In God's eyes there are no Iron Curtains, Purple Curtains, Bamboo Curtains—there aren't Communists or Capitalists—just people with needs and hopes and aspirations, people who need to feel the warmth of God's love as they see it through our loving actions.

This I believe is Paul's message for you and me in these verses. To sit idly by in comfort on our cushioned pews while people die from hunger, terrorism, disease, or battle is to miss the deepest meaning of our faith. It's true, of course, there aren't easy answers and the task is so big it seems almost hopeless. But what answers there are, even in the confused and complex world of today, must be found by the people of God—the Church.

Practical Words for Church Leaders.

Paul next directs his comments to certain rules that apply to the elders—leaders—in the church at Ephesus (5:17–20). And as happens most of the time, what was important teaching in the first century has its application in the church of the twentieth century.

You will recall that the elders, as the term is used here, were the leaders—the preachers, teachers, and administrators—in the local church congregations. It would appear from the wording in verse 17 that some of the leaders had their own means of financial support. But there were also those who did not have outside means of support and were dependent on the church for their income. And so the first of Paul's instructions here is that these leaders were to be adequately paid, "...worthy of double honour" (5:17). And then in verse 18 the Apostle substantiates his instruction by writing "For the scripture saith."

Paul's first quotation, "Thou shalt not muzzle the ox that treadeth out the corn" is taken from the Torah (Deut. 25:4). Here we have a word picture from ancient times when grain was threshed by oxen walking back and forth over it until the kernels were separated from the stalks or the ears. At such times the oxen were to be left free to eat as they worked. After all, unless the threshing beasts were adequately fed they couldn't function satisfactorily.

The second quotation Paul uses to justify his instructions carried the authority of Jesus Himself, "The labourer is worthy of his reward" (Luke 10:7). The idea Paul wants Timothy to understand here is that the church leaders (elders) are to faithfully discharge their responsibilities and they are to receive proper remuneration.

Adequately paying the leaders of our church congregations in no way commercializes their ministry. In order to serve their people most pastors find themselves "on duty" twenty-four hours a day. Yes, their service is "unto the Lord," but to be effective, they must have the resources to be physically and emotionally prepared. Happily, I think the day is long passed when congregations had the weird notion that if they kept the pastor poor, he would remain humble. And no longer do we equate spirituality with being poor.

The implication here for us as Christians and as part of God's new society, the church, is to be proper stewards of our resources. It is part of our Christian service to support financially the work of the Lord and His servants in a way that will make possible the movement of the gospel into the hearts and lives of our neighbors across the street and across the world.

The Apostle's next words give every indication of being directed to a problem that had arisen in Ephesus, but it also has a familiar sound to us today (5:19–20). Apparently, there were those making accusations against their leaders. In responding to this problem Paul reminds Timothy that Jewish Law forbids accepting any accusation except on the

Accusations Made against the Leaders.

59

evidence of two or three witnesses (Deut. 19:15). But then he goes on to write that if an accusation is substantiated by proper witnesses, the leader is to be disciplined, "Them that sin rebuke before all, that others also may fear" (5:20).

I think there are two things that are important to us here. First, loose accusations, charges, criticisms, gossip violate the message of Jesus and of the ancient Jewish Law in which we are told that we are to love others—our neighbors—*as we love ourselves*. Idle criticism and gossip about our leaders is destructive. Rather, as brothers and sisters in the Lord we are to affirm, to build up, to pray for one another. If we are encouraging and praying for our leaders—even when they may not see things just the way we do—it isn't likely we will be sniping at them and making false accusations against them.

It is true, of course, that from time to time someone in a leadership position will be guilty of sin that calls for rebuke. At such times Paul makes it clear that Timothy is to act in a decisive manner so that others may realize the necessity for being faithful to Jesus' teaching.

Following along immediately in the same mood, Paul gives Timothy some important personal advice—he is to be impartial in his treatment of those leaders who are under his charge (5:21). The importance of this advice is reinforced with the words that it is "before God, and the Lord Jesus Christ, and the elect angels" that this instruction is given.

Paul was expressing a powerful truth to the Christians of his time and to ours. Preferential treatment for political or social reasons is unbecoming in the work and ministry of the church. The Good News of Jesus Christ finds everyone equal in the eyes of God. In another place Paul worded it this way, "For there is no respect of persons with God" (Rom. 2:11).

God does not judge a person on the basis of personality, the outward display of success, or social status. Who we know doesn't matter; it is *what we are* that counts. Each of us is gifted; we are all important to the Lord and to His work. Some are gifted as teachers or preachers, others have talent for administration, and still others, like some ladies in the church where I work, have the gift of ministering to elderly women. There are those who cook for Meals on Wheels and others who deliver the hot food to housebound and deprived people.

A view of the Triumphal Arch of Galerius, which straddled the Via Egnatia at Thessalonica. On Paul's second missionary journey Timothy was with the apostle and Silas on their trip from Philippi to this important city. Mention is also made of another of Timothy's visits to Thessalonia when he was sent there on a special mission for Paul (1 Thess. 3:2).

A group of women in my church make some of the most beautiful Christmas stockings that I've ever seen. These are treasured by all who have them as a labor of love for the Lord and the people of our town. The point is that we all have talents that are important to God, and no one within the church should be looked on as being more "influential" and useful in the Lord's work.

Don't Be in a Hurry.

In verse 22 Paul writes, "Lay hands suddenly on no man." This seems to be a repeat of the teaching expressed in Chapter 3. The idea here seems to be that Timothy is not to be in a hurry to commission anyone for service until they have been trained and tested. Again, we get the notion here that while we are to be affirmers and encouragers, we must be cautious not to push new Christians especially into places of leadership until they are more mature.

The next phrase in verse 22, "...neither be partaker of other men's sins: keep thyself pure" may refer to the importance of not commissioning someone for leadership whose motives are not pure. And this, of course, underlines the importance of going slow and giving training. Or Paul may be advising Timothy to exercise his leadership cautiously, knowing that his actions and decisions won't necessarily please everybody. He needed to avoid the temptation of going with the majority—he wasn't to become involved in "other men's sins," but he was to be a pure example as a leader-witness for Christ.

A Personal Word for the Young Leader.

Throughout this letter so far and in Paul's other writings we see that Paul and Timothy had far more than a professional relationship. They were close friends and companions—brothers in the Lord. This certainly comes through now as we sense Paul's concern for the physical well-being of his young friend (5:23).

Paul well understood the strain and stress Timothy was feeling as he undertook the heavy responsibility of leading the Ephesian churches. So often the give-and-take of human relationships within the church exacts a heavy emotional toll for the sincere believer. And so, within the cultural norm of the first century the Apostle advises Timothy to "use a little wine for thy stomach's sake" as a means, possibly, of enhancing his digestion.

As Christians whose bodies are the temple of the Holy

Spirit, it is important that physical care not be ignored. Neglect dulls our physical and emotional capabilities. Our physical welfare is important; our bodies are to be fit if we are to have the energy and sharpness essential to effective living and witnessing.

While there is much that we don't know about Paul, maintaining his physical and emotional health must have been a lesson he learned well in spite of his "thorn in the flesh." He traveled thousands of miles over rough country on foot in all kinds of weather. His experience included physical abuse, hardships of all kinds, and shipwrecks. Yet he always had the stamina to press on. It would seem none of that would have been possible unless he was thoughtfully attentive to the needs of his physical well-being.

Our Actions Are in God's Hands.

Finally, in these closing words of Chapter 5, Paul either creates or quotes an aphorism about good deeds, sins, and ultimate judgment that will be of help to Timothy in his oversight of the Christians and the churches under his care (5:24–25). In our relationships with other people we know that some sins will be readily recognizable and others will be unseen or hidden. At the same time the good deeds of some people will be readily apparent while the good deeds of others may not be recognized or applauded. But these are matters that are best left up to God, for He is the ultimate judge of sin and rewarder of good.

This is a hard lesson for all of us to learn. In our relationships in general and especially in our church relationships we have an inveterate desire to set things right, to be the judge of what is right and what is wrong. But there are those times when we are to rest easy and leave the judgments up to God.

Advice for Christian Slaves and Masters.

As Paul brings to a close this particular part of our lesson on how the church should function, he directs his attention to slaves and masters in first-century culture (6:1–2). It has been estimated that there were between 50 and 60 million slaves throughout the Roman Empire. And while our King James translation of these verses uses the term "servants," the Greek word that was used could be translated "slaves."

From Paul's perspective Christian slaves were to work for their human masters as if they were working for God.

This was an important point for Paul because some of the unrest among slaves was evidently credited to the Apostle's teaching.

It was true, of course, that the Good News states that through faith all people everywhere are free from the bonds of sin and death and the demands of the Law. But it also teaches that commitment to God and our neighbors are characteristic signs of faith.

Paul taught both of these ideas, but I suspect hearers then were like hearers today—they heard only the part they wanted to hear. The slaves "heard" that in Christ all are free. They may even have heard or read Paul's words, "Be not ye the servants of men" (1 Cor. 7:23), and interpreted it quite literally—doing everything they could to get themselves free, including escape. But this caused Christianity to be ridiculed among the Roman slaveholders as a subversive doctrine.

What the Apostle was actually teaching was that a person who had dedicated his life and work to God, even if he is a slave, is *free in spirit* and no one man can own him. Quite naturally, Paul's words here should never be taken as supportive of slavery or any other form of human abuse. Rather, they teach that compassion and love and dedication to God are to be the primary motivators of our behavior. Throughout his missionary travels Paul had taught a gospel of justice and equality for everyone, and that is precisely what he wants his young protégé to teach and preach.

False Teachers.

Now as Paul moves toward the close of this intensely warm and personal letter to his young friend, he brings together some final thoughts on sound teaching and proper behavior.

He first turns his attention to those false teachers who were trying hard to disrupt the Christian unity in the church (6:3–5). And in verse 3 Paul contrasts their efforts with true teaching, "The words of our Lord Jesus Christ, and…the doctrine which is according to godliness." Any other teaching is false and disruptive.

These false teachers prided themselves in their clever arguments and sophisticated rhetoric. They enjoyed parading their Gnostic wisdom and wrangling over meaningless fine points—all as a means of avoiding the authentic issues of a life that is centered in Jesus Christ.

It is critically important that we not get sidetracked with petty arguments and pointless details in our pilgrimage of faith. Such a hollow and shallow preoccupation can turn us from being true witnesses to the freedom that is ours in Christ. It is a tragic waste for Christians to drain off vital energy in pursuing the trivial. Paul's warning to Timothy is clear, "From such withdraw thyself" (6:5).

Evidently the false teachers that Paul was warning Timothy about were, among other things, involved in commercializing their message, "...supposing that gain is godliness" (6:5). But the Apostle moves on now to insist that it isn't the "gain" of material possessions that gives life meaning. Rather, the "great gain" in life comes through "godliness with contentment" (6:6). And the meaning of "contentment" as Paul used it here refers to having so much that we don't need anything else. And the "so much" refers to an "all sufficiency" in Christ and not to anything material.

Love of Money.

In verse 7 Paul reminds Timothy that "we brought nothing into this world, and...we can carry nothing out." He also reminds his young friend about the temptations that plague the wealthy, and then comes that much misquoted verse, "For the love of money is the root of all evil" (6:10). At no point, of course, does Paul imply that making money or having money is wrong. But the great temptation is to love it to the exclusion of everything else.

Now, most of us are not troubled with having too much money. So it is easy for us to shrug our shoulders and pass this verse off lightly. It doesn't matter, though, whether we have a little money or a lot, if we make it the number one value in our lives—if we're willing to relegate relationships and God to second place, we "have erred from the faith, and pierced...through with many sorrows" (6:10).

Paul next pleads with Timothy not to fall into this trap as he writes, "But thou, O man of God, *flee these things*" (italics mine). The Apostle's language is dramatic and vivid. Timothy is to dash away from any concentration on material gain and give himself over entirely to "righteousness, godliness, faith, love, patience, meekness" (6:11). In these words Paul asks Timothy to concentrate all of his energy on lasting and permanent virtues—on the wealth of God through Jesus Christ.

Paul continues now with vivid and aggressive language

Fight the Good Fight of Faith.

as he literally commands Timothy to "Fight the good fight of faith, lay hold on eternal life" (6:12). I'm not sure whether the Apostle is using an athletic or military metaphor in this verse, but whichever it is we catch his meaning. We are to be aggressive in our pursuit of faith in the confidence of the future life in Christ.

Closing Words of Advice.

Following Paul's soaring charge to Timothy (6:13–14), the Apostle's language reaches new heights in the marvelous doxology and description of Jesus as "The blessed and only Potentate, the King of kings, and Lord of lords" (6:15). And then it seems that he is too inspired to stop. Yes, the letter is over, but here are a couple of additional thoughts.

Paul's first afterthought is for those people in Ephesus who are wealthy. Perhaps he didn't want them to misunderstand his earlier comments (6:17–19). He urges them to use their wealth wisely and with compassion. Above all they are to put their trust and love in God and not in their money. And they are to use their wealth for the work of the Lord.

Paul's second afterthought focuses in on his young friend. His love and concern come through with every word! He urges Timothy to keep his spiritual priorities sorted out. It isn't picking at fine points of interpretation or lofty arguments that witness to the Good News of life in Christ. Rather, it is a day-by-day surrender of our priorities to God, and a living out of Jesus' teaching at home, in the office, at the supermarket—wherever we meet people with a need.

The Church Is a Family.

But there is no way we can be authentic witnesses in the marketplaces of the world out of an isolated environment. It is from the nourishing that comes from our church family that the gospel is spoken and acted out in the world.

Paul knew and understood this as he wrote to Timothy. That is why the instruction and advice in this power-packed little letter have lived throughout the centuries. Since you and I are the church, the Apostle's message in this letter is for us. May we always be as generous with the giving of ourselves as Christ was with the giving of Himself.

Heavenly Father, Help me to live out the teachings of Your Son. It's hard to "turn the other cheek," "love my enemies," or not see the mote in my brother's eye. Help me to submit daily to Your Way—to be a light—wherever I am. AMEN.

WHAT THIS SCRIPTURE MEANS TO ME—1 Timothy 5–6

My grandfather was a tall, taciturn Texan who had been a cattle drover in his younger days. He ate heartily but was always a little on the gaunt side. That his metabolism did not pass down the gene route to me is something I mourn with every consumed calorie.

I'm sure his six daughters didn't confuse him with God, but Papa's word was law—not a despised law but an accepted, good-for-you kind of law. He provided more than adequately for his family. We all knew he loved us, but I never heard such a sentiment actually expressed. His comments were terse and to the point, with not one wasted word.

I have a picture of Papa holding me when I was two. Instead of looking toward the camera, I had twisted around in his arms and was looking intently, wide-eyed, up at his face. That's the way it was with Papa. Then and later he was very much a stack pole in my life; we just didn't talk much about our feelings.

When Paul wrote to Timothy, "Rebuke not an elder..." I thought immediately of Papa and how none of his family needed to be reminded to be respectful. And as I read again the words of advice Paul gave Timothy about his relationship with different groups of people—caring for the "real widows," paying the preacher, those with an excessive love for money—my thoughts drifted back to a letter I received from my grandfather during my first year in college.

I was a very homesick freshman and was worried about my grades. I had written Papa and shared some of my feelings. Then I had gone on to reminisce a bit about my fond memories of going to his house after school and studying by his black wood stove until my father picked me up on his way home from work. I wrote about how much I had enjoyed his afternoon treats—roasted field corn from the top of the wood stove or a pomegranate, a Japanese persimmon or a big purple fig, depending on the season. Other times it would be soft, pastel-colored marsh-mallows from a tall glass jar on the clock shelf. It was the kind of letter a lonesome girl would write to someone she loved very much.

I really didn't expect an answer to my letter so I was surprised when Papa's letter came and even more surprised at its newsy, philosophical and almost chatty contents. This what he wrote:

> Dear Gran-daughter
>
> Your letter of Feb 5 came last week. Glad to have it. You asked if Margret was still cooking good. Yes—she would kill me with grub, if I would furnish it. And eat it. My garden stuff came up but the birds are eating it up. Guess I will have a job planting it over. The early bird did not get the worm this time. I notice you doubt making good grades this term, don't show *white feather*. So I sign my name, yours cordially, affectionaly, truley, and sincereally
>
> Papa Rice

Paul wrote to Timothy, I feel, in such a caring fashion, and I can understand their warm relationship in a new way as I reread Papa's letter, the only one that I know of in the family. Paul's letters to Timothy are just as unique in the detailed expression of concern between a mentor and his student, a father-figure and his son, two fellow Christians in the strong bonds of God's love.

Of course, Paul's letter dealt with larger, more serious problems of the church, but when my grandfather's letter came, there was nothing more serious for me than survival scholastically and emotionally.

Paul completed his letter by writing movingly, "O Timothy, guard what has been entrusted to you...some have missed the mark as regards the faith (6:20–21; RSV). And I read a like concern from "I notice you doubt making good grades [missing the mark] this term, don't show *white feather*."

What does this Scripture mean to me? My feelings come alive to a new sense of the deep relationship between Paul and Timothy when I reflect on my grandfather's concern for me. Paul is not preaching to Timothy or giving him a doctrinal lesson; he is writing out of a heart of love—Paul really cares about Timothy!

And then, his conclusion, "Grace be with thee. Amen," reads warmly to me as I hear the echo from a forty-year-old letter, "So I sign my name, yours cordially, affectionaly, truley and sincereally, Papa Rice."

LESSON 4
2 TIMOTHY 1–2

A Challenge to Serve

Abba Father, Thank You for Your power, love, and sound mind. When I'm tempted to feel powerless, unloved, and emotionally unglued, I can seize Your Word and gain strength from its truths. Amen.

We are now beginning our study of what we know as Paul's second letter to Timothy. It is highly possible he wrote many other letters to his young friend, but these are the two that have been preserved for us in Scripture.

This second letter to Timothy is very special because it may be the last time these two close friends communicated with each other. And even more important, it is likely this is the last letter the Apostle ever wrote. Somehow we catch a tone of finality in Paul's words. Then, too, we pick up a sound of quiet confidence that he has accomplished his mission for God. And while we can't know for sure, it seems that he may have felt his death was near.

As we read this letter, we can know that we are working our way through the noble Apostle's final words of wisdom. From the time of his conversion many years before, Paul had worked tirelessly as a missionary carrying the Good News wherever he went. He had been an eloquent and able apostle and a Spirit-guided interpreter of the Christian faith. And now, as he looked back over the events of his life, he felt assured that to the best of his ability he had followed the direction and leading of the Lord.

Paul wanted to leave his "son" Timothy and the church a challenge to continue witnessing and acting out the teachings of Jesus. And so we find in this letter words of encouragement, warning, and advice.

As we move through this short letter, we can readily sense the concern Paul had for the church and for Timothy, his "son" in the faith. At the same time it isn't hard to imagine some of what Timothy may have felt as he read the lines and between the lines of this letter. There could be no mistaking the meaning of Paul's words toward the end of the letter, "For I am now ready to be offered, and the time of my departure is at hand" (4:6). Certainly, the signals were clear to Timothy, even as they are for us, that this particular letter has special meaning.

The Salutation and Greeting.

Once again, Paul follows the traditional first-century pattern—he immediately identifies himself as the writer and Timothy as the intended reader. And once again, in identifying himself he stresses his position as an apostle of the Lord.

This salutation (1:1–2) seems to have added significance because in it he uses the term "Jesus Christ" and "Christ Jesus" three times. It seems likely that Paul wants to impress one more time on young Timothy that the Christian faith as a Way of Life is Jesus Christ and nothing else.

And it is because of Jesus Christ that Paul is an apostle whose compelling mission is to witness to the grace of God. In writing to the Corinthian Christians Paul worded it this way, "Woe is unto me, if I preach not the gospel!" (9:16). But we don't sense from any of Paul's writings that his intense desire to witness is forced upon him in any way. Rather, he does so willingly because, as he wrote Timothy in the first letter, "Godliness is profitable unto all things, having *promise of the life that now is*, and of that which is to come" (1 Tim. 4:8, italics mine). In other words, Paul cares for his work and ministry passionately because he finds in it "the promise of life."

I firmly believe that we can find "the promise of life" in the fulfillment of our own particular vocation and calling as well. Unfortunately, though, the word "work" in our culture so often takes on a negative connotation. Time and time again I've heard it expressed this way, "Work is what we have to do in order to be able to do some of the things we want to do." This is a sad outlook on work because it implies that we spend most of our time plodding along, gritting our teeth through daily routines so we can spend a few hours on the weekend or on vacation doing what we really want to do.

This certainly wasn't Paul's attitude! Even with the hardship of first-century travel and the opposition of critics and the frustration over the stumblings and bumblings of new Christians, Paul always seemed to feel the excitement and adventure in doing what he knew he was supposed to do.

Once again the Apostle models for us an attitude toward life that is important. Whatever vocation we seem to be "called" to is honorable and is to be enjoyed. In fact, perhaps the strongest witness any of us can give to our family and our neighbors is one that shows life in Christ as an exciting adventure of growth and maturity.

Next, in just a very few words, Paul assures Timothy of his prayers and of his confidence in the young man and in his faith (1:3–5). I'm sure that as Paul languished in his Roman prison cell, he was able to visualize his young friend moving along the streets of Ephesus and witnessing to his faith in the churches and in the city's agora. Such pictures enabled the Apostle to pray with special insight.

Timothy Is in Paul's Prayers.

At the same time it doesn't stretch the imagination too far to visualize Timothy's reactions as he reads these words and knows that in a far-off prison cell his "father in the Lord" is praying daily for him. Of course, Paul longs to see his young friend (1:4) and, of course, Timothy longs to see the face of his spiritual mentor. And, while that is impossible, both know they can fellowship together in faith through prayer.

I'm sure you've had the experience, as I have, of knowing that someone was praying for you at a time of particular need. Remembering that, we can understand a little of what it must have meant to Timothy to be assured of the prayer support of his beloved friend.

Then as Paul reflects on Timothy's life and service, he further affirms his friend's faith by comparing it to that of his mother and grandmother (1:5). He seems to be reminding Timothy that as a third-generation Christian, he has a great faith heritage in these two Godly women. In these words, I believe Paul is saluting the Christian family. Many of us are indebted to the faithfulness of our Christian parents, from whom we get the inspiration to guide and nurture our own children in the ways of the Lord.

"Stir Up the Gift of God."

The Apostle then moves on to remind Timothy of the gifts God has given him, and in doing this he uses an expression that has lost somewhat its full meaning by the translation, "stir up the gift" (1:6). Instead of "stir up," the Greek word Paul used created a vivid word picture reminiscent of a fire that has died down a little, and which is then rekindled by stirring with a stick or poker. The stirring causes the sparks to fly as the fire flares up and burns with new vigor.

Again the imagery and the application is startling. The Christian life is not meant to be a complacent existence. The flame of our gifts, abilities, and actions is intended to burn brightly, to take the stirring of change and new things, so that our lives send out sparks that ignite spiritual fire in others.

While we don't know for sure the meaning of Paul's words in verse 6 about the "putting on of my hands," it is possible the reference is to an earlier act of ordination or commissioning that recognized Timothy's gifts. But whatever is meant, these words were a grand expression of affirmation of the young man's abilities.

Then Paul's insight and rhetoric, as he reminds Timothy of the attributes that are his as a leader, reach new heights. These are powerful words: "For God hath not given us the spirit of fear; but of *power*, and of *love*, and of *a sound mind*" (1:7, italics mine). As Christians, our gift from God is power coupled with love and good judgment—it is this that needs to be "stirred" continually.

Don't Be Ashamed to Witness.

Paul builds block upon block of advice as he moves on now to urge Timothy to never be "ashamed" or timid or hesitant in his witness for the Lord (1:8). And to that he adds, "Nor of me his prisoner." It is possible there were those in Ephesus who were discounting Paul's leadership and effectiveness because of his age. For his time the Apostle was now an old man, but he was persistent in his teaching and preaching in spite of either age or imprisonment. It is possible they thought him to be an eccentric old man who wouldn't retire. We sense here that Paul may be aware of such criticism, and so he asks his young friend not to be ashamed of him.

There was a time not long ago when we were obsessed with a youth culture. Retirement was forced or mandated early if at all possible. But in more recent years a new mood is sweeping across our society. We are finding a new respect and reverence for the experience and insight that age can bring. And the result in business and in the professions and in church life is an enrichment and a quality of life that is invigorating to our culture. One of the greatest privileges of the young is to draw on the experiences and insight and wisdom of older Christians.

Paul now in verses 9 and 10 gives an awesome and comprehensive summation of God's Good News: God "hath saved us, and called us with a holy calling, not according to our works, but according to his own purpose and grace..." (1:9).

A Grand Summation of the Gospel.

These words may well express the single most important idea in Paul's understanding of God: Without limit, God's grace is available to everyone! But that grace, Paul insists, is a gift of God and there is nothing we can do to earn it. This is the gospel: God saves us; He calls us. And then in verse 10 we are told that through Christ the grip of death is released and we have LIFE now and always through Jesus Christ.

It is no wonder that Paul could write about God's grace with such passion. He remembered, I'm sure, that he was one of the major persecutors of the church when it was first formed. But by God's grace he had been transformed from an impassioned and hateful enemy of Christians to the great missionary and interpreter of the gospel of Christ. It is obvious in all of Paul's writings that he never stopped marveling at the grace of such a God. It was the focal point of his life as he witnessed continually to the truth that God's grace, as expressed in the life, death, and resurrection of Jesus Christ, *is the gospel!*

In this part of our lesson (1:11–14) Paul is writing about his own call to be a preacher, an apostle, and a teacher to the gentiles—non-Jews—and then he turns his attention to Timothy's call. However, in a very real sense, what is said here is practical for each of us.

A Call to Service.

After defining his own personal call in verse 11, Paul

73

then refers to what it has cost him. When he writes, "I also suffer these things," we have a grand understatement here that is elaborated on elsewhere. A rather vivid description of what it had cost him to be a preacher, apostle, and teacher is found in 2 Corinthians 11:22–33. But that isn't the point he wants to emphasize here. Instead he moves right on to assure Timothy that he is not concerned with hardships or rejection because his confidence and trust are firmly fixed in the Lord (1:12).

Then in verses 13 and 14 Paul has some special words of counsel for his young protégé—he is to follow Paul's model of "sound words"—sound teaching. But then Paul adds a most important condition—he is to stand firm for the truth "in faith and love which is in Christ Jesus." In other words, I believe the Apostle is telling Timothy—and us—to stand firm for the truth as we understand it, but *in love and faith in Christ*. This should temper our attitude greatly toward those whose standards and doctrinal understanding are different from ours. Paul's words here seem to rule out the anger and hostility that characterize so much of our relationships with Christians who are "different" from us.

False Acquaintances and a True Friend.

In the closing verses of what we know as Chapter 1 of this second letter to Timothy, brief mention is made of three men (1:15–18). All three—Phygellus, Hermogenes, and Onesiphorus—were from Ephesus, the capital of the Roman province of Asia in the western part of what was then known as Asia Minor. Apparently, the first two men mentioned (1:15) had at one time been close friends of Paul, but had since deserted him, along with certain other Christians, because of the stigma of his imprisonment in Rome.

The third man, Onesiphorus, is a different story, though. It is likely from Paul's wording here that this man and his family had often entertained and cared for the apostle when he was in Ephesus. But of greater importance, we learn from these few words that when Onesiphorus heard of Paul's imprisonment, he traveled the long, weary miles from Ephesus on the east coast of the Aegean all the way west to Rome just to see his friend and minister to him. Then upon his arrival in the teeming city of more than a million people, he persisted until he found where the Apostle was imprisoned. And now Paul writes that "he oft refreshed me, and was not ashamed of my chain" (1:16).

It would be easy in our reading and study to pass quickly over these four verses. After all, the three men are mentioned nowhere else in the New Testament, and we don't know anything more about their lives. But in this brief portrait of one of the men we find a moving story and a model of what it means to be a true friend in Christ.

Here was a man who had befriended Paul during the

Ruins of Corinth with the Acropolis in the background. It was to Corinth that Timothy and Silas came to report to Paul about the progress of the Christians in Thessalonica. Scenes such as this in their original splendor would have been familiar sights to young Timothy.

height of his effective ministry in Ephesus. But it is clear from what Paul writes here that Onesiphorus had been an intimate and caring friend—not only in words but in action. It was also a friendship that was active and vital when things weren't going well, even weathering Paul's imprisonment.

In the friendship of Onesiphorus and Paul we see a live, first-century picture of Jesus' words when He gave a special blessing to certain people as He said, "I was an hungered, and ye gave me meat: I was thirsty, and ye gave me drink: I was a stranger, and ye took me in: Naked, and ye clothed me: I was sick, and ye visited me: *I was in prison, and ye came unto me*" (Matt. 25:35–36, italics mine).

In this one-time mention in our Scripture lesson of this otherwise unknown man we have a model for Christian discipleship today. In a society that makes it difficult to maintain close friendships, we all need friends like Onesiphorus to support us. But equally important, we need to be an Onesiphorus to our fellow Christians.

Instructions to Teach. Paul now moves ahead to give Timothy some very practical instructions for his continuing ministry in Ephesus. First, he is to remain strong in his faith, and second, he is to teach what he has learned to others so they in turn can continue and expand the process (2:1–2).

The training of people for service in the church has always been a formidable challenge, but it is one that must be met in every generation. Paul knew that if the Good News about life in Christ was to move out across the world, people needed to understand the message so they could teach others. And the marvelous thing about Paul's instruction given here around the middle of the first century is that it started a chain reaction that has never stopped.

Our home study classes, our Sunday schools, and Bible studies like this one we are doing now are a continuation of Paul's instructions here for Timothy to pass on to others what he had been taught so they could pass it on to many more.

The point is that you and I as Christians are a part of this whole process whether we clerk in a store, work in a professional office, keep house as a wife and mother, or are a commercial airline pilot. We are all Timothys and students of Timothy. But in reality all of this began when Jesus selected twelve laypersons—regular folks like us—and taught them during the three years they traveled and lived together. During that teaching experience He sent them out from time to time with the Good News, and then following His resurrection and the coming of the Holy Spirit, the gospel flame has moved out across the world.

From the very beginning the Christian faith has been a contagious movement as it has spread from individual to individual and from small group to small group. Unfortunately, as time has passed, we have become guilty all too often of thinking that the Christian message and mission are to be carried on by professional people—ordained clergypersons or specially trained people with college and seminary education. And, yes, there is a place for these formally trained leaders and teachers, but they are never intended to take our place as day-to-day witnesses of what God has done for us and of what He is doing in our lives now.

But we must always remember that the mission of the church—and we are the church—is to teach and train Christians to be productive followers of Christ. First, we need to learn all we can and then we have something to pass on along with our personal experience.

Paul next elaborates on his "be strong in the grace of God" theme by giving Timothy three word pictures, which surely had meaning for him, but we, too, can identify with them to a certain extent. The first is that of a soldier, "Thou therefore endure hardness, as a good soldier of Jesus Christ" (2:3–4).

Be Strong in Grace.

Soldiers then and now are often called upon to endure hardship in the course of duty. Let's face it, though, in spite of some of the pop psychology and cheap-grace theology that assaults us these days, life isn't particularly easy for anybody. As Christians we are continually caught in the tug-of-war between what is good and what is not. But as faithful members of Christ's body, the church, we are to be strong, like soldiers, in our resolve to follow Jesus' teaching, whatever the cost.

For me, the second word picture Paul draws here is of a master craftsman (2:5). It is true that many of the later translations connect this verse with an athlete who is competing in a contest. But I believe the application is equally appropriate for a master craftsman or an artist who is striving to do the best possible job.

Recently, I had the opportunity to spend an afternoon

with Henry Wedemeyer, a renowned sculptor. In discussing his craft he told me that creativity is like the angel in Michelangelo's marble that was just waiting to get out. But it took skill to release the angel—to be creative—skill that took years to master. For the uninitiated, the artist's and craftsman's efforts look easy, but in reality that skill can come only from years of laborious effort and pain.

The third word picture is that of a farmer (2:6). To be successful in the first century as well as in the twentieth century, a farmer or rancher must be hardworking and determined to persevere against what at times may be adverse and frustrating conditions.

In each of these pictures—of the soldier, of the master craftsman or athlete, and of the farmer—we catch the mood of endurance and discipline and hard work, but also there is the mood of achievement, of satisfaction, and of hope. In this superb montage of pictures we find a great source of strength for our Christian pilgrimage.

The Heart of the Gospel.

Paul now builds on the pictures he has drawn and the instruction given so far by directing Timothy's attention to Jesus, "Remember that Jesus Christ of the seed of David was raised from the dead according to my gospel" (2:8). The Apostle readily recognized the unpopularity of this message, for in another place he had said it was blasphemy to the Jews and folly to the Greeks. But Paul wanted to remind Timothy one more time that Jesus Christ is the heart and center of the gospel—the Jesus who became human as "the seed of David," but whose divinity was attested to by His resurrection from the dead. It is this Jesus we serve and represent in the world.

We can be certain that Paul himself gained strength by remembering Jesus Christ and His victory over sin and death. I'm sure as he languished in his Roman prison cell, it was his memory of Christ that enabled him to handle the suffering and the hardship (2:9–10). For the great Apostle the cost was high, but he wanted Timothy to understand that the goal was well worth the price.

In a way, this scene reminds me of a twentieth-century Christian martyr, Dietrich Bonhoeffer, who launched a powerful attack on "easy Christianity" in his book *The Cost of Discipleship*. This German Christian was a brillant theologian, a gifted preacher, and a creative thinker whose life was thoroughly committed to Christ. But his message ran counter to the goals of Nazi Germany in the late 1930s and early 1940s. He opposed Hitler vigorously and was imprisoned. And then just before Germany's final defeat in 1945, Bonhoeffer was executed—he gave his life for the ideals of the gospel. The cost of Bonhoeffer's discipleship was his own life. And the cost of Paul's faithfulness to his calling as an apostle was to be his life. It was this absolute commitment that the aged apostle wanted Timothy to understand.

A Hymn of Faith.

Through this part of Paul's letter he has been reminding his young friend of his mission for Christ and he has been remembering and reflecting on the Lord Jesus. Now, he apparently breaks out into a hymn (2:11–13)—a hymn that celebrates faithfulness even though the going may be hard. The lyrics remind us that if we are faithful in our commitment to Christ, He is faithful in His commitment to us. But there's more—He is faithful even when we aren't.

The hymn connects pairs of ideas that may be seen as an action based on our commitment to Christ and His response to that action. If we are committed enough to follow Him in death, then we will live with Him forever.

Then the hymn takes a turn to give us a warning, "If we deny him, he also will deny us: If we believe not, yet he abideth faithful" (2:12–13). Here the pairing of patterns breaks down and we see the immeasurable love of God at work. He is ready to accept us at *any* time as our Redeemer and Lord. This is the message Paul wants Timothy to pass on to his hearers in Ephesus (2:14).

Handle the Word of Truth Properly.

Instead of spending valuable time debating senseless topics, Paul urges Timothy and the whole church to be faithful to the Word of God (2:14–19). His words in verse 15 have challenged Christians from Timothy's time to ours, "Study to shew thyself approved unto God, a workman that needeth not to be ashamed, rightly dividing the word of truth."

To the people at Ephesus, this was a warning not to get sidetracked by the philosophical trends and elaborate systems of fables that were taught as "secret knowledge" by the false Gnostic teachers. And to make certain the deception stops, Paul mentions the names of two of the false teachers (2:17).

Stately ruins in the Greek city of Corinth. It was from Corinth that Paul wrote the letter to the Christians at Rome. Timothy was with the apostle then and is mentioned in the closing verses (Rom. 16:21).

The application of this part of our lesson is important. The Good News of the gospel of Jesus Christ is a simple message: God loves us; He has given us grace and redemption through Christ; He has called us to live Christian lives in response to that grace by loving Him and our fellow human beings. And we know that our hope for the future is centered in Him and His mysterious will.

As with the Ephesian Christians under Timothy's care, it is important that we focus on the heart of the gospel as Paul has given it to us here and not complicate things with a lot of speculations. We are often confronted with "profane and vain babblings" in our day under the guise of

Christian teaching. There are those who try to chart God's movements now and in the future and who attempt to identify without question those who are faithful and those who aren't. But the truth can only be "rightly divided" as we study *in love* under the leadership of the Spirit.

Then comes the great assurance. No matter what anyone may think, "The Lord knoweth them that are his" (2:19). On one hand I find it comforting that God knows His own—on the other it is a sobering truth. God looks on the heart of every person. He knows our intentions and our motives. There's no mask we can put on that keeps Him from seeing the real us.

The Lord Knows His Own.

Throughout all of Paul's writings he makes it clear that our spiritual life is between God and ourselves. We are responsible to Him alone, and we are not to be slaves to the opinions of others. At the same time, though, we are not free to hurt others with our "freedoms." Christian love respects the faith and feelings of others and is always careful not to offend anyone.

But Paul hasn't said it all yet because then he adds that we are to "depart from iniquity." We are responsible to turn our backs on sin and evil.

The Apostle moves on in his thinking now and uses a different metaphor (2:20–22) to clarify the point of his message. Here he pictures a house in which we find a variety of utensils. Each one has its purpose. But, of course, if a utensil is broken or deteriorates from use, it serves no purpose and is worthless.

Vessels of Honor and Vessels of Dishonor.

Then, too, some of those utensils are made of gold or silver, while others are made of wood or clay. Some are used for good and noble purposes; others are not.

While no word picture is perfect, it appears Paul is still referring to false teachers and people in the church. Then as now, any institution, including the church, is composed of all kinds of people. The search for the perfect church always ends in disillusionment. The important thing for us to understand is that judgment is to be left to God. And to move from the image to the truth of the image, we are to "depart from iniquity" and keep ourselves pure and valuable for God's service. Then we will be "a vessel unto honor" and "prepared unto every good work" (2:21).

"Flee Also Youthful Lusts."

Becoming a vessel of honor—one valuable for use by the Lord—is Paul's challenge to these Ephesian Christians and us. Now he has a special word for young Timothy, but it is also very pertinent for us, "Flee also youthful lusts" (2:22). This admonition is thought to go beyond what are generally considered to be sexual sins. Rather, the reference could be to a lust for success or honor or power.

The warning to Timothy and to the Ephesian Christians and to us is to run from any desire or ambition that makes our life in Christ secondary. Instead, our sole focus is to be on "righteousness, faith, charity, and peace." But again Paul warns about getting sidetracked by "foolish and unlearned questions...knowing that they do gender strifes" (2:23).

A prime example of "foolish and unlearned questions" surfaced in the Middle Ages in the long-standing argument among theologians as to how many angels could stand on the head of a pin. Extreme? Yes! But I sometimes wonder about some of those arguments and practices that can so easily sidetrack us today and cause us to be impotent in our witness to the world.

Instruct with Gentleness.

In the closing verses of our Scripture for this lesson we catch once again a glimpse into the tender heart of this great apostle. He tells Timothy that as Christians and Christian leaders we "must not strive" (2:24). Rather, the Christian is to be "*gentle* unto *all* men" and "patient" (italics mine).

This same spirit continues in verses 25 and 26 as Paul tries to help his readers see that if we patiently and without arrogance present the truth, even those who may disagree will be uplifted by an authentic display of Christian love. It is important, I think, that we understand there will be differences of opinion and diversity within the fellowship of believers, but if we deal with each other *patiently and gently and in love*, these differences will not reach the fever pitch of strife and bitterness.

In this lesson Paul has issued a challenge to Timothy and the church of all times to follow his example as a witness and minister of the gospel of Christ. Following Paul's conversion he evidently went into seclusion for quite some time where he was able to reflect on all that had happened to him and to listen to the Lord. Then we see him in Jerusalem where he was able to converse with and learn from those who had traveled with Jesus during the three years of His ministry. And undoubtedly his early days in Antioch with Barnabas were times of learning as well as serving.

From this we see that even Paul's dramatic meeting with Jesus on the Damascus road apparently didn't qualify him to rush out to witness or assume a leadership role in the Christian community. And so once again this great apostle is our model for preparedness—for studying so that our witness and service is effective and "approved unto God." And with that background Paul next turns his attention as he writes Timothy to the importance of preparation for service.

Father, Striving comes so easily in today's world of competition, stress, hurry, and worldwide distress. Help me to see Your hand in everything—even in situations that tempt me to quarrel and be troubled. Help me to see things more and more from Your point of view. Amen.

WHAT THIS SCRIPTURE MEANS TO ME—2 Timothy 1–2

Every now and then George and I laugh about the first meal I cooked after we were married. I opened a can of pork and beans, stuffed two eggs, and made a fruit salad of one apple, a half orange, and a banana. Finally, I toasted four pieces of bread—and was a nervous wreck.

Oh, yes, George reminds me; we had olives, too, from a box of goodies brought over by a friend as we were moving into our student apartment.

If, at that moment, I could have seen stretched out end to end all the chickens, roasts, sauces, soups, pies, cakes, cookies, potatoes, and beans I was to cook in the next 39 years, I would have thrown up my hands in absolute and utter despair and gone back to Mabank.

Happily, in those early days we had a butcher in the meat market at the corner store where I bought our groceries who taught me how to cook a roast. I read cook books, asked friends for recipes, and gradually, one meal at a time, I became a pretty good cook. We had to eat! And I had to hang in there to learn to cook.

When Timothy unrolled Paul's parchment to the words, "Thou therefore endure hardness, as a good soldier of Jesus Christ" (2 Tim. 2:3), I would imagine he was tempted to roll it up and tuck it on a shelf to read later. He knew the kind of prison Paul was writing from, and Paul certainly was not quiet about the times he had been dragged before the authorities to be beaten, imprisoned, or shackled!

Paul was the trailblazer, the church builder, the pioneer who first preached a bold new gospel. Timothy would never be that kind of pioneer—just as I will never be a Julia Child—but he was making the start of his pilgrimage where the church was at that time. And he most certainly would be called upon to "endure."

Endure, that's the word for Timothy as he deals with Hymenaeus and Philetus, who were real problems in the church even though they didn't abuse Timothy physically. And Paul went on to instruct young Timothy to endure by holding his tongue, studying to preach well, and to be an "apt teacher" in order to keep the church from wandering off in the wrong direction.

We have belonged to the same church for 35 years. In fact, George and I met in its basement at a college department Sunday morning breakfast. He says he is going to stay at that church until he gets even!

In superficial ways our church has gone through several changes, and at one point I just was not ready to accept some of those changes. In my panic I took two offices in an organization that had far outlived its usefulness, became anxious and sleepless, and thought the whole thing was going down the drain.

Fortunately I had a friend who helped me gain a new perspective. In essence he told me the same thing that Paul said to Timothy about enduring as a good soldier. The advice I got was something like this, "Hang in there, Katy. Don't give up. Stay in the boat!" And then he explained to me the ancient symbol of the church, a boat sailing on rough seas.

"And," he added quietly, "give God back his church."

I have been moved deeply by the stories of Christian martyrs who have had their hands chopped off rather than renounce the gospel, or who have been tied to posts in some city square and burned to death. That sort of suffering is hard to imagine. I wonder if, however, in the drama and intensity of a once-in-a-lifetime situation where the only answer is a single yes or no, we ordinary Christians could not have risen to the occasion.

The mucky part is living one day at a time with other struggling Christians in a fellowship that we need so much and where we are sure to have to work through differences, hurt feelings, and individual growth spurts all fifty-two weeks of the year.

Is it possible that enduring can in a way be equated with being stood against a wall and shot for the glory of God? Do we dare take hope and feel that in the *enduring*, we join with the great Apostle Paul in suffering with and for our Lord instead of feeling guilty that for us there are no firing squads by which to measure our faith? In fact, Paul's suffering at the time of his writing this letter had boiled down to *enduring* that prison one day at a time.

I am greatly encouraged by these words, "And the servant of the Lord must not strive [be quarrelsome]; but be gentle [kindly] unto all men [everyone]...." Tough! but gentle...and one day at a time.

LESSON 5
2 TIMOTHY 3—4

Preparation for Service

Gracious Lord, Prepare me for the work that You have called me to. Use all the moments of my days to mold me and make me into a vessel of honor for You. AMEN.

All of us are called to be witnesses and to serve in the name of Jesus Christ. And preparation for that service is most important if we are to be effective.

We need not only spiritual preparation, but we need knowledge and training for the particular jobs to which we feel called. We should also be perceptive and wise in the ways of the church and the world in which we live. Jesus understood this when He told His disciples that in their ministry they should be "wise as serpents, and harmless as doves" (Matt. 10:16).

In this last half of Paul's letter to Timothy, which makes up our lesson now, we find some specific instructions from the Apostle to his young disciple. There were wise words here for him that also apply graphically to us in this latter part of the twentieth century. As Christians, our primary purpose in life now is to work with and serve our brothers and sisters in the Lord, and to witness to the Good News of Jesus Christ to our neighbors wherever they are.

Troubled Times Ahead.

An important part of our preparation for service is to be keenly aware of what is going on in the world and in the church. After all, as followers of Jesus we may not be *of* the world, but we are most definitely *in* the world, and the people who are to be the object of our attention and service are also *in* the world. For this reason we are to be alert to world events and needs in order to properly represent Christ. Then, too, it is in the midst of the real world that the power and love of God can be best seen.

Paul's warning is clear, "This know also, that in the last days perilous times shall come" (3:1). Unquestionably, the Apostle knew that this warning would not come as a surprise to Timothy, but he wanted to emphasize it one more time—he wanted to remind his young friend of something they had probably talked about many times.

What did Paul mean by "last days" and "perilous times"? It doesn't seem likely here that he was referring to the end of time as we know it. Rather, I suspect from Paul's perspective the reference was to that broad expanse of time between Jesus' first coming and His Second Coming. In other words, the "last days" are now for the church in every generation.

And as for the "perilous times," Paul's original wording was very strong. The opposition can be fierce as Christians attempt to live their faith in a hostile world. For Timothy and the first-century Christians the opposition became extremely violent. The Roman and the Greek world vigorously opposed the Christians' refusal to conform to pagan customs. Yet it was during this time that the Good News penetrated the known world.

In our twentieth-century world physical opposition to Christianity has been minimal in western society except for during World War II, in Europe, when Christian opposition to Hitler and his demented lieutenants created martyrs among leaders and followers alike. Yet even during the apparent comfortable times there have been emotional pressures and opposition that tested severely the Christian witness.

But in some parts of the world today there are Christians caught in the violent grip of "perilous times." The restrictions on the Christian life and witness are extremely vigorous in parts of Asia, in many Third World countries, and in the Communist bloc.

Yes, we too live in the "last days" when only those who are serious about their commitment hold steady to their faith. Others, like the troublemakers in Ephesus, try to undermine the true gospel, or just leave the church and are contemptuous of those who try to practice the teachings of Jesus in their daily lives.

A List of Evil Traits.

Then to make sure that Timothy has a clear picture of why the times are troubled and perilous, Paul lists some twenty traits characteristic of people who are in opposition to the Good News (3:2–5). As we examine this list we can't help but be impressed with just how up-to-date it is. While expressions and technology have changed drastically in 1,900 years, people have remained pretty much the same.

Reference is made here to people who are egocentric, grasping for what others have, and boastful and arrogant. At the same time these people are ungrateful and irreverent—focusing on pleasure instead of on God and Jesus Christ. There is a reckless unconcern for truth and love and proper values. And while many of these people put up a good religious front, they are in reality traitors to the faith and completely lacking spiritual power.

A Form but No Power.

The Apostle recognizes that there are those who have "a form of godliness" but are without power (3:5). What he has just described form the ingredients of what we've come to know in our time as a "me first" society, in which the primary emphasis is on acquiring money and means for personal gain and pleasure and worldly power. It is these egocentric ones who lack spiritual virility and strength because of their concentration on the wrong things.

The religious climate at the time of Jesus was rich in traditions and practices that had been in existence for hundreds of years. The Jewish people respected the Law of Moses, but they eventually became so caught up in the traditions that they became slaves to them. The purposes of the Law and their religious traditions were completely lost. Obeying the traditions became more important than justice and concern for others.

But the message of Jesus called them to a radical change in their religious commitment. He certainly understood their problem when he said, "Full well ye reject the commandment of God, that ye may keep your own tradition" (Mark 7:9). And in another time and place, as He stressed the more important matters of love, justice, and an authentic encounter with God, He said, "These ought ye to have done, and not to leave the other undone" (Matt. 23:23). The Good News of Jesus Christ has the power to change individual lives—and the world—if we do not hide behind "a form of godliness."

In the last ten years or so we've seen a rather remarkable increase in church attendance and in Christian activity. In many places churches are growing at a rapid pace. And it has become quite fashionable to speak of one's religious experience and church affiliation. At the same time we are seeing a growing expression of Christian responsibility in the social and political arenas.

All of this is good. Jesus insisted that His followers are to be "salt" and "light" in the world. We are to give flavor and illumination to the world around us. But even while this is happening there are those with "a form of godliness" who insist that a certain point of view is Christian and any variation from that is wrong. These same people frequently label their position on a given social or political issue as *the* Christian one with the implication that to disagree is unChristian.

It would appear, too, that in the first century as well as today there may be those who use the church and their relation to it for personal gain. Their commitment is not to Christ and His church, but to enhancing their own cause.

And so Paul is warning Timothy that any distortion of an authentic witness to Jesus Christ is to be avoided because it is a form of godliness without the power. He knew that if Christians then and now are to discern what is real as opposed to what is merely a "form," we will need to be intensely aware of what is going on around us and have Spirit-directed insight and *preparation*.

To further emphasize the importance of preparation and spiritual discernment, Paul next refers to what must have been a particular problem in the Ephesian church (3:6–7). While we're not privy to all the details, it would appear

A Warning against Troublemakers.

89

that some rather fast talking false teachers had gotten to some of the women in the congregation and the truth was being confused. Paul's comment that they were "ever learning, and never able to come to the knowledge of the truth" is quite revealing (3:7).

I don't believe Paul is suggesting that any of us ever have a *full* knowledge of the truth. But there comes a time when we must act on the truth we have. We've probably all known people who were "professional students." They spent all their time pursuing some learning fad or reality, but never acted on the truth they had. It is this kind of person that can easily be led astray, and that is evidently what was going on among a few in Ephesus.

A view of the Colosseum from the Roman Forum. Even before his first visit to Rome Timothy's name was familiar to the Christians there. Paul also mentions Timothy being with him during his imprisonment.

To illustrate his point Paul refers to two men, Jannes and Jambres (3:8–9). Actually, these two men are not mentioned anywhere else in the Bible, but Hebrew legend and certain intertestament writings identify them as the Egyptian court magicians who opposed Moses and Aaron when they appeared before Pharaoh (Exod. 7:11). There is even the suggestion in some ancient writings that these two men became so fascinated with the God-given powers that Moses and Aaron exhibited that they joined the Hebrew hordes that left Egypt and continued their opposition of Moses in their attempt to lead people astray. But they were not successful, and Paul compares them now to those false teachers in Ephesus whose "folly" would be exposed.

The Example of Jannes and Jambres.

Paul next directs his attention to his young protégé in the gospel (3:10–13). Without any taint of destructive ego the Apostle sets himself up as an example in "doctrine, manner of life, purpose, faith, longsuffering, charity, patience" (3:10) as Timothy will inevitably confront the hardships and persecution that will come because of his faith.

Paul's Example.

After all, Paul had endured a great deal of persecution, and he specifically mentions his experiences in Lystra, Iconium, and Antioch, which are graphically told by Luke in the book of Acts (13:13–14:20). These incidents would undoubtedly have been quite familiar to Timothy since Lystra was his hometown.

No one could ever doubt that Paul had endured a great deal of hardship for his faith. He had been jailed many times, beaten, stoned, left for dead, and even shipwrecked—all because of his allegiance to Jesus, "but out of them all the Lord delivered me" (3:11). And the implication now is that Timothy will be put to severe tests in his work for the Lord, "Yea, and all that will live godly in Christ Jesus shall suffer persecution" (3:12).

The lesson for us in these words is that we can expect difficulties as we are faithful to the very practical teachings of Jesus. The way of love and patience and integrity may not always be understood by those with whom we must deal every day. A spirit of love and justice irrespective of race or culture is frequently misunderstood. And to care actively for the hungry and deprived and suffering in places where the political and social ideology conflicts with ours is not likely to be popular. Even today, as in the first century, faithful Christians are confronting hostility and suffering, but we hold the same promise that Paul did—the Lord is with us.

Sound Preparation for Service.

Paul continues his personal word to Timothy (3:14–17) by urging him to remain faithful to all that he has learned. Timothy had been taught "the holy scriptures" from early childhood, and from them he had learned about God and His plan of "salvation through faith which is in Christ Jesus" (3:15). While Timothy was not blessed, as we are, by having the New Testament, he had been well taught in the Old Testament Scriptures by his faithful mother and grandmother. And it is this that forms the foundation for Timothy's life and service.

Many of us, I'm sure, are a lot like Timothy. We have grown up learning Bible stories in Sunday school. We've heard the Bible read at home and in church, and from that we've learned of God's love and of salvation through Jesus Christ. As we've grown and matured, our understanding of biblical truth has expanded and has had an even greater influence on our lives. And it is through this preparation that we have been made "wise unto salvation."

Next Paul gives Timothy and us some of the most important words in this letter, "All scripture is given by inspiration of God, and is profitable for doctrine, for reproof, for correction, for instruction in righteousness" (3:16). Paul's original wording tells us that Scripture is "God breathed"; it is God's teaching!

Over the years teachers and interpreters of Scripture have at times expanded and theorized on all that these words mean. Paul, in his infinite wisdom and under the direction of the Holy Spirit, let his words stand as we have them here. The Scriptures are indeed our source for spiritual teaching. From them we have words of caution and reproof, as well as instruction in righteousness. Furthermore, as that last phrase in verse 17 suggests, we have the Scriptures so we will know how to act out our faith, "That the man of God may be perfect, thoroughly furnished unto all good works." The Bible is the book of our faith; without it we cannot be equipped for effective service and ministry. With it, we are well prepared for service that builds up the Church, the Body of Christ.

As the tired and aged Apostle moves toward the close of this letter, he seems to sense that these may be his last words to his young friend. He knows so well the burden of leadership that is about to descend on his protégé. For some thirty years Paul has witnessed to his faith in Christ under the most difficult of circumstances. His legacy is about to be shifted to Timothy, and so he writes, "I charge thee therefore before God, and the Lord Jesus Christ…" With these words I get the feeling that what he is about to write now is very important.

Paul's urgent word of instruction to Timothy comes through now loud and clear: "Preach the word" (4:2). For Timothy, the Word was the Old Testament Scriptures and the teachings of Jesus as he had learned them from Paul and others. He was always to be prepared to witness and teach. I understand Paul to be saying two things here to his young friend: Always be ready to speak about your faith in God, and always be true to the Good News of Jesus Christ.

Proclaim the Good News.

Next, the Apostle instructs Timothy to "be instant in season, out of season." This Old English terminology may be a bit confusing to us, but in effect Paul is telling Timothy there is a great urgency to his witness and task as a leader in the church. Paul knew that as the overseer for the churches in Ephesus and Asia Minor Timothy would be traveling a great deal in visiting the congregations—he must always be alert and ready to preach and teach.

Like Timothy, we too are called to proclaim our faith—to witness to what the Lord has done in us. We are to be alert to opportunities and feel a great urgency to fulfill our role as Christians. And a vital part of our preparation for that role is that we prepare and study the Word of God and always be faithful to it irrespective of the response.

In verses 3 and 4 the Apostle warns Timothy and us that at times people will not listen—they will resist commitment to Christ because it seems too hard, and they will look for an easy way, an easy gospel. At such times, teachers of cheap grace—of an undemanding gospel—may become popular and attract considerable attention. In fact, Paul says there will be those who "turn away their ears from the truth" in favor of fables or myths that demand nothing from them. But the Apostle's instruction to Timothy is to hold steady, "Preach the word…exhort with all longsuffering and doctrine" (4:2). In other words, Timothy wasn't to be swayed by the popularity of false teachers or those who watered down the gospel. Rather, he was to remain faithful to God's Word.

A Personal Application.

Paul's "hold steady...be faithful" charge for Timothy has an immediate application for us today. The temptation comes to all of us to let down on our commitment to Christ and to teach and follow a gospel that may be more popular because it doesn't insist on obedience to Jesus' teaching. We may be tempted to take the easy way in our desire to be accepted and popular. But as with Timothy, these are temptations that are to be firmly resisted. The Christian way isn't particularly easy; it is a way of commitment. But as we hold steady, we can receive encouragement in this assurance from the Lord, "Come, ye blessed of my Father, inherit the kingdom prepared for you from the foundation of the world" (Matt. 25:34).

During my maturing years in the church I have had the opportunity to learn from some able teachers. But some of the best advice I've received has come at unexpected times and from unexpected sources.

I was working one summer as an assistant in a rather large church, and my primary assignment was to visit the sick and elderly in the local hospitals and nursing homes. It was in one of the nursing homes that I met Mr. Simpson and his wife. Mr. Simpson was a very old retired minister, and during our visits he often told me stories about his own life and ministry. But on our last visit, before I returned to school, Mr. Simpson became my "Apostle Paul." His last words to me were a challenge I've never forgotten, "Jim, we've done a lot of talking together this summer. You've come to know me, and I think I know you. Now, I want to give you one piece of advice before you go.

"It's the same advice I was given when I first entered the ministry. I've tried to follow it all of my life, and I've had a wonderful life and ministry. If you follow it, you will, too. It's a simple lesson, but never forget it—Preach the Word and love the people."

Then Mr. Simpson held up his old worn Bible and continued, "You can make a lot of mistakes in the church. But if you always preach the Word and love the people, you'll get along fine."

"Preach the Word"—be faithful in your witness for the

Lord. This worked for Paul during his thirty years of missionary activity. It worked for Timothy at Ephesus and for Mr. Simpson in Texas. It has worked for me, and it will work for you, too.

Paul now concludes his final instructions to Timothy by saying, "Do the work of an evangelist, make full proof of thy ministry" (4:5). For Paul, the work of an evangelist was the sharing of the Good News of Jesus Christ. The word *evangelism* comes from a root word that means to herald or proclaim the gospel.

Unfortunately, we have come to associate evangelism

The Importance of Evangelism.

Paving stones in the old Roman road that leads into the Forum. According to tradition, the prison in which Paul was at least some of the time held was adjacent to the Forum. Sights such as this were familiar to Timothy during his time there.

with the professional clergy. But this is every Christian's task—our task. During the early days of the Christian church the gospel moved from person to person by word of mouth. All Christians were evangelists. But between the fourth and the beginning of the sixteenth century much of the early ardor had cooled. Christianity became institutionalized and people were "born into the church" as it were.

But with the Reformation of the sixteenth century a new vigor swept into the church. The work of evangelism again came into its own. The flame of commitment to life in Christ burned brightly again as Christians moved out across the world to witness to their faith. And the great missionary movements of the eighteenth and nineteenth centuries brought the gospel to the new world, and then it spread to Asia, Central and South America, and the islands of the Pacific. And the fires of evangelism are burning brightly today, especially in Africa and other Third World countries.

For many of us, though, our opportunities for evangelism, for witnessing to what Christ means to us, are right in the neighborhoods and towns where we live. It is here that we are to speak of and act out our faith in shops and offices and in traffic and in school. But our effectiveness and commitment draw strength and power as we put into practice the advice that Paul gave his young protégé in this letter.

"I Have Kept the Faith."

Paul's reverie at this point is poignant as he acknowledges that his death is probably very close. His reflections are voiced in the athletic metaphors that are so much a part of Paul's letters as he writes, "I have fought a good fight, I have finished my course, I have kept the faith" (4:7). I'm sure young Timothy must have nodded his head in agreement as he read these words. He knew his mentor well. He knew the Apostle's strengths as well as his weaknesses—Paul had fought hard and he had kept the faith, and he had always kept going, "I press toward the mark for the prize of the high calling of God in Christ Jesus" (Phil. 3:14).

I don't sense in these words of Paul that he is boasting or on an ego trip. From the time of his conversion more than thirty years before he had "endured," he had pressed on and fought a good fight for his Lord. And now, as he looks back, he sees it all as good—and he's ready for whatever comes.

Now comes the great affirmation of Paul's confidence in God (4:8). God had been faithful throughout all of his struggle, and he knew that God would continue to be faithful. As he had written earlier in this very letter, "I know whom I have believed, and am persuaded that he is able to keep that which I have committed unto him against that day" (1:12).

"A Crown of Righteousness."

Again, in speaking of the "crown" of righteousness, Paul slips once more into an athletic metaphor as he visualizes the wreath that was awarded the winner in a race. This is what he saw as being his from the Lord—not because of what he had done but because of his faith in Jesus Christ.

From here through the rest of the letter (4:9–22) we have a very human portrait of Paul. First, he expresses the desire to see Timothy one more time as he writes, "Do thy diligence to come shortly unto me" (4:9). And as if that isn't enough, he repeats himself, except this time he is more specific, "Do thy diligence to come before winter" (4:21).

The Apostle's Last Words.

And then in verse 11 Paul asks Timothy to bring Mark with him when he comes, "for he is profitable to me for the ministry." We discovered at the end of Paul's earlier letter to the Colossian Christians that a healing had occurred between the Apostle and Mark. You will remember that Paul refused to let Mark go on the second missionary journey because of his desertion on the first trip, and that he and Barnabas separated because of this crisis.

We don't know what happened between that time and the writing of the Colossian letter. But we do know that reconciliation occurred, and Paul now acknowledges once again Mark's importance to him. In these few words we get a brief glimpse of how fruitful service can emerge out of a past failure—what a marvelous affirmation of the grace of God!

Then in verse 13 comes another personal request as Paul asks his friend to bring a coat that he had left behind at Troas "and the books, but especially the parchments." I like that. The Apostle wanted the refreshment that he knew his books and parchments would bring. Like some of us, I suspect Paul was a first-century bookworm.

The Apostle then gives his young friend one last warning as he urges him to watch out for Alexander the coppersmith, who "did me much evil," and then he speaks of those "friends" who apparently failed to stand by him at his first trial in Rome. This may well be a warning to Timothy that this same sort of thing can happen to him. But again comes the assurance that through all of this "the Lord stood with me" (4:17–18).

Finally, almost reluctantly, Paul draws the letter to a close as he sends greetings to old friends and in turn he gives Timothy greetings from certain friends in Rome. And the letter closes with the Apostle's last benediction, "The Lord Jesus Christ be with thy spirit. Grace be with you. Amen" (4:22).

Throughout this important letter we have seen again and again the importance of our being prepared for Christian service. Paul's instructions have been concise and clear, even in the midst of the urgency he felt. At the same time the Apostle has given us the assurance that God is always faithful in being with us and for us. As always Paul is the Grand Encourager; he is our model for Christian witness and service today.

My Father, Thank You for Your faithfulness and great strength. Thank You for never leaving me, for the triumph I have over every evil attack, for Your abundant peace and love. Amen.

WHAT THIS SCRIPTURE MEANS TO ME—2 Timothy 3–4

When our children were young and we had to be away for a few days, my mother would come to stay with them. Since she was from a tiny little town in East Texas, mother always felt a bit edgy about driving through the unfamiliar streets and heavier traffic in our town.

And ususally, at least once during her stay, she would find herself driving the wrong way on our one-way streets. When this happened, our perfectionist ten-year-old daughter would slide down to the floor of the car in the hope that none of her friends would see her.

Since my mother's gift of child-caring was fairly stressful for her, I tried to plan ahead to make it as easy as possible for her. I prepared meals in advance, and I made lists—lists of piano lesson schedules and routes to the teacher's house, which clothes the children should wear to school, church activities, Bluebird meetings, and menus.

All of this flooded back into my mind when I read Paul's list at the close of his second letter to Timothy:

1. Come quickly
2. Bring Mark with you
3. Bring my cloak
4. Bring the books
5. Bring the parchments, especially
6. Tell Prisca and Aquila and Onesiphorus' household hello
7. Come before winter

Paul, of course, was writing from prison. He was looking forward to the warmth of his cloak, fellowship with Luke and Mark, his close friends, the companionship of his books, and parchments for his letters. Undoubtedly he sensed that death was near, so these were important days for the weary apostle.

In another letter Paul had written, "I have learned, in whatsoever state I am, therewith to be content" (Phil. 4:11). Now, I'm sure that his contentment came from a knowledge that he had served the Lord for many years and that he could spend time with dear friends and his books—even in the unpleasant atmosphere of a Roman prison.

Many years ago we had a dreadful siege of red measles at our house—both our little girls had them at the same time. To make the hours pass more quickly and to avoid complications that might occur if they strained their eyes, I spent a great deal of time reading aloud to them. We all got caught up in the ventures of the Five Little Peppers and other stories, as the girls snuggled up against me. There was much about that red measles seige that was unpleasant, but all of us have happy memories of being together and experiencing the stories in our imaginations.

Difficult experiences can include moments of real human communion. So often the warmth of human fellowship can give encouragement in our hard times. Perhaps your father is having his third surgery in eighteen months, and you think, "Oh, no! Not the hospital again!" But then a friend comes by and takes you down to the coffee shop for a steaming bowl of soup. You sit and talk awhile, and even laugh together. Your world is a little brighter because a friend cared.

Or, you return home from the cemetery after the funeral of a loved one to find family and friends gathered to ease the pain of lonely moments. In the midst of sadness, there is reinforcing, heart-stirring family joy. People hug each other and laugh and cry at the same time.

I have a friend who was an Associated Press reporter at the Auschwitz trials in post-war Germany. He told us this was the most difficult assignment he ever had. During the course of the long trial the judges, the jurors, the prosecution attorney, and members of the press developed a lasting bond of friendship. And forty years later he still keeps in touch with many of the witnesses who had survived the death camp. They, too, had established close friendships, which had their beginnings when he would take them home to dinner after a long day in court. There they cried together, releasing their tension and fear, but, he said, "We laughed, too."

Auschwitz was the demonic culmination of Paul's list of warnings in 2 Timothy 3:1–4. Evil and sin were very present then as they are now, but Paul's words to young Timothy apply equally well to our day. We are to continue steadfastly in our faith, knowing that we are not alone. Like Paul, we can find encouragement in the warmth and fellowship of our books and our friends.

LESSON 6
TITUS 1—2:10

Order in the Church

Dear Heavenly Father, Let me not be one of the number that claims to know You, but by works—life-style, attitude, value system—deny You. Mold me into Your own likeness. AMEN.

We move now in our studies to the short letter of Paul to Titus. Along with the two letters to Timothy we have just studied, this letter speaks directly to the struggles of the early church for identity and order. Throughout the Roman world the growth of the young churches was rapid. New converts from Judaism and the pagan religions of that time were banded together in fellowship. Guidance and direction were needed in terms of personal faith and church order.

If we compare this letter with the two addressed to Timothy, we find some similarities between this one and the first one to Timothy. Here Paul discusses qualities of leadership, coping with false teachers, and the basis for Christian behavior.

Speculation has been rampant over the years as to when this letter was written. I tend to join with those who believe this letter preceded the writing of the two letters to Timothy. Others position Titus between the two letters to Timothy. But in a sense, this is not of major importance; it is the contents that were urgently needed by the first-century church and that give us direction in our Christian life and community today.

Before we move into a closer study of this letter, I want to address myself to this question, "What can we gain from a study of this old and short letter that will give us direction today?"

For me, there are two important reasons for our study of this letter. First, we have an urgent need for a clear understanding of Scriptural truth, and we need to know how to relate that to the mission of the church. Today the Body of Christ across the world is composed of many individual denominations and churches, most of which are organized quite differently. I don't see this as a weakness, but rather as a strength. It is important, though, that the leadership be well prepared, and the qualification for leaders and their preparation remain pretty much the same now as when Paul wrote these letters.

Second, we have in this letter some vital teachings of Christian faith and doctrine that are timeless. Paul's words of instruction on how a Christian is to behave are amazingly up-to-date.

A Letter from Paul, a Servant of God.

The opening words follow the custom of the day in that, as he has done in his other letters, Paul identifies himself as the writer (1:1). And for reasons probably best known to Paul he identifies himself as "a servant of God" instead of a servant of Jesus Christ as he has done in other letters. That, then, is followed immediately by the declaration of his apostleship.

The Apostle obviously felt the need at the very beginning of this letter to underline the authority that was his based on what he was about to say. But I like to think that he first identified himself as "a servant of God" to help Titus and his other readers to see that he was, in fact, one of them. We are all "servants of God"—sinners saved by grace through faith in Jesus Christ. And we are all called to witness to what God has done for us. In that respect, we are all alike. As Paul wrote to the Roman Christians, "For there is no respect of persons with God" (Rom. 2:11).

I recall the story of a famous doctor who lived during the Middle Ages. He spent his life among poor people, helping them as best he could. He lived with them, ate with them, and dressed as they did. He was "one of them."

LESSON SIX

But one day he became very ill and was taken to what we would refer to today as a charity hospital. As his condition deteriorated, the doctors decided not to try to save him because of the seriousness of his illness. In Latin, the medical language of the day, the doctors were discussing his condition as they stood around his bedside. One of them said, "What is the use to try to save him. He is just one more useless beggar."

This comment penetrated the confusion of the patient's mind, and he responded as vigorously as he could in scholarly Latin, "Call no man worthless for whom Christ died."

The point, of course, is that we today rank with the great apostle as servants of God—important to Him and important in the mission of the church. This is just one more reason Paul's words here are significant for us.

Paul, an Apostle.

As he has in other letters, Paul identifies himself immediately as an apostle—one sent by God. And while he was not one of the original twelve who had traveled with Jesus, his confrontation with the Lord on the Damascus road gave him the position and authority he needed to fulfill his mission to the first-century church as the "apostle to the gentiles." Again, this reminder had a purpose—he spoke with authority, and he wanted them to listen.

A Basis for Paul's Authority.

The Apostle establishes his authority next, "according to the faith of God's elect, and the acknowledging of the truth which is after godliness." Faith was then and is now the standard for the Christian. But faith is not a statement of creed. Rather, it "is after godliness"—it becomes authentic when acted out daily in Godly action.

In other words, Paul is stressing right at the beginning of this letter that holy living, Godly action, is indeed the test of faith—Godly action as expressed in love and caring concern in every compartment of our lives. This was Paul's standard for his own service, and it is to be ours as we witness to the Good News today.

Paul continues his opening words of greeting by speaking of our "hope of eternal life" that was "promised before the world began" (1:2). This promise of life in Christ now and throughout all of the endless unknown of the future is the very heart of the Christian message. It was to this message that Paul gave his entire life after his conversion.

103

And it is this same message that is to be at the heart of our witness.

"To Titus....."   As we have seen in our study of Paul's writings, for the most part his letters were addressed to a church at a certain place—to a group of Christians who lived in a particular city or area. However, this letter, like the ones to Timothy we have just studied and the one to follow in this series of lessons, is addressed to a person. In this case the person is Titus (1:4).

Titus, a Greek, was one of Paul's disciples and traveling companions, "Mine own son after the common faith." But

A view of the theater, the agora, and Harbor Way in Ephesus. As overseer by appointment of Paul to the Ephesian church, the bustling streets of Ephesus were most familiar to Timothy.

actually we know virtually nothing about him except what Paul tells us in his second letter to the Christians at Corinth and in his letter to the Christians in Galatia. Beyond that Titus is mentioned just in passing in the second letter to Timothy. And he is not mentioned at all in the book of Acts.

It was Titus, a gentile convert, who was with Paul and Barnabas when they defended their ministry to the gentiles at the Jerusalem Council (Acts 15). Some of the Jewish Christians felt that Titus and all gentile converts should submit to the Jewish Law, including the circumcision of males. But Paul was insistent that Titus did not have to become a Jew in order to be a Christian. For Paul, the grace of God was sufficient for everyone. The Apostle stood his ground at that historic occasion, which later resulted in the Jewish Christian leaders agreeing that indeed the Holy Spirit was at work in the lives of the gentile Christians, and they didn't need to submit themselves to the Jewish Law.

Then in 2 Corinthians we learn that Titus was entrusted by Paul with the delicate job of delivering a rather stern letter to the church at Corinth. On that occasion he served as Paul's envoy to the Corinthian Christians with the result that later their mutiny against the Apostle was resolved and they once again acknowledged his authority.

The Mission in Crete.

With this background of successfully completed assignments, it is understandable that the Apostle once again gave to Titus an important mission. Paul's instructions were clear: He was to establish order in the churches in Crete—"Set in order the things that are wanting"—and then appoint competent leaders—"Ordain elders in every city, as I had appointed thee" (1:5).

This was an awesome task. Crete was a large Mediterranean island located southeast of Greece. It was a beautiful and historic place. The ancient and highly advanced Minoan civilization had flourished there some 1500 years earlier. And in the eighth century B.C., the Greek poet Homer referred to Crete as the island of 100 cities.

There had been a Jewish colony on Crete for several hundred years, and Christianity may well have been introduced to Cretans in the earliest days of the faith. Luke mentions that there were people from Crete in Jerusalem who heard the gospel through Peter's sermon on the Day of Pentecost.

But for all of its beauty and history, Crete was known throughout the ancient world as a place of great moral corruption. In fact, Paul quotes one of their own leaders in verse 12, "The Cretans are always liars, evil beasts, slow bellies [lazy]" (1:12), and then he goes on in the next verse to say, apparently out of his own knowledge, "This witness is true."

All of this simply meant that Titus' job and that of the other faithful Christians in Crete would not be easy. And then, as if the moral corruption on the island was not enough, the Jewish Christians were evidently teaching that a person had to become a Jew and submit to Jewish Law in order to be a Christian. This, of course, was the very thing that Titus had seen Paul fight so successfully against at the Jerusalem meeting (Acts 15).

We would say today that Titus had two strikes against him in his ministry on Crete: Christianity wasn't particularly popular on the island, and as an uncircumcised gentile, he wouldn't be accepted by the Jewish Christian community.

There is somewhat of a parallel to the obstacles that face us in our twentieth-century witness for the Lord. While we're not necessarily confronted by Jewish customs and rituals, there are those Christian legalists who at times insist that only their way is right and everyone else is wrong. And the moral attitude that prevails in so much of society is hostile to the teachings of Jesus. As with Titus, our task, if we are faithful to it, is not particularly easy.

But, back to Titus and first-century Crete. Paul commissioned Titus to establish a semblance of order, of structure, of program, so the Christian church could function in unity. Next, he was to select and train leaders to conduct the work of the church. Then, as now, if we are to proclaim and witness to the Good News of Jesus Christ, we need training. This does not apply solely to the ordained leadership in our churches. We are, one way or another, all leaders. Our task is to represent the Good News by word and action. We—you and I—are the church, the Body of Christ in our world. And our mission is to minister to the material and emotional needs of people as well as to their spiritual needs.

We are to constantly work together in order and unity—

to study, as we are now, to become leaders in the work of the church. And then we are to apply ourselves, as Paul did, to be mentors—encouragers—of others so they may become effective ambassadors of Christ.

The model for leadership in the Cretan church (1:6–9) is virtually identical to what Paul gave Timothy in his first letter, and it bears repetition. Qualifications for authentic leadership were the same in Crete as in Ephesus—and they remain the same in your town and mine today.

Leaders are to be devoted, without any kind of hidden agenda, to the work of the Lord. Their marriage and family life are to be modeled after the teaching of Jesus. Values are to be Godly, and their habits are to be temperate. And above everything else a leader is to hold "fast the faithful word as he hath been taught, that he may be able by sound doctrine both to exhort and to convince the gainsayers" (1:9). Paul is saying here that, as leaders, we are to have a sound understanding of our biblical faith. This will enable us to teach "sound doctrine" to others and to refute the unsound arguments of false teachers.

False Teachers.

Having just given us the characteristics of a good leader, Paul next turns his attention to a brief description of those false teachers and leaders in Crete who were creating problems (1:10–14). It isn't Paul's intention here to publish the names of the troublemakers and unsound teachers. Rather, he wants Titus and us to recognize them by a description of their actions.

He first describes them as being unruly—undisciplined—loose talkers whose word could not be trusted and whose lives were corrupt. They were "deceivers" in that they did not speak the truth, but by their words and actions they actually led people away from the truth. And it appears from Paul's words in verse 11 that these false teachers were disrupting family life, "teaching things which they ought not." Furthermore, they were guilty of asserting their leadership and unsound teaching "for filthy lucre's sake"—it was being done for financial gain.

But to heap tragedy on tragedy, we get the idea from verse 10 that the false teaching and teachers the Apostle is denouncing here were largely from among the religious Jews, "They of the circumcision." There are now, as there were then, those who want to complicate the simple teaching that Jesus Christ lived, died, and burst out of the grave on that first Easter morning to provide salvation to everyone who will follow Him.

Paul's plan of action against these false teachers is very clear, their "mouths must be stopped" (1:11). The original wording that Paul used here is obscured by the abruptness of the phrase. Yes, their mouths were to be stopped, but not just by *any* means. They were to be silenced by reasonable argument, with an attempt to win them rather than to demolish or destroy them.

I think Paul's implication here is important to us. Yes, we are to stand firm against sin and evil, but we must always be sensitive to the importance of trying to win people to Christ who are themselves sinful. There is a big difference between attacking sin and attacking the sinner. As Christian witnesses our task is to win people, not drive them away and silence them by any form of attack method.

In addition to the opposition from false teachers among the Jews, Paul's use here of a 500-year-old quote about Cretan character (1:12) certainly indicates that opposition to Christian teaching was also coming from the Cretans themselves. Because of the foul reputation these islanders had, the Apostle felt it was especially important that a clear line of demarcation be drawn between the true and the false.

"Unto the Pure All Things Are Pure."

Paul moves on now to further describe the heresy that was polluting the Cretan church (1:15–16). When he writes, "Unto the pure all things are pure: but unto them that are defiled and unbelieving is nothing pure," we catch a further clue into the situation confronting Titus. I think here Paul is speaking about the living of life from two perspectives—one of genuine faith, and one of genuine fear.

The Christian who lives a life of faith trusts God—trusts His forgiveness in the face of human imperfection while at the same time he or she trusts in the grace and love of God. There is an almost naive and innocent quality to genuine faith that is less concerned with boundaries. The person of genuine faith does what is right and good because he or she loves God and not out of fear of breaking rules.

The second perspective is that of fear. This person is constantly afraid that he or she will make God angry. The "God will get you" shadow is paralyzing. It keeps people from trusting and loving God and from trusting and loving themselves. Spontaneity is lost because of a slavish attempt to obey rules. For this person the Scriptures are a rule book rather than a love story about the love and grace of God.

The point is—there's nothing slavish or legalistic about loving God out of a heart made pure by a simple and passionate faith in Jesus Christ. And this genuine love finds expression in loving actions toward our brothers and sisters in Christ and toward our neighbors wherever they are.

It is true, as Paul writes, that to the pure of heart and mind, all things are pure, but to those who have permitted themselves to become impure and defiled by unbelief, nothing is pure. And Paul's description of the impure is scathing. They are rebellious, repulsive in their disobedience, and useless to God.

"Harbor Way"—the street that lead from central Ephesus to the harbor. During Timothy's years in Ephesus this was a busy thoroughfare.

Christian Guidelines. Paul's mood shifts now as he lays out some practical instructions to Titus (2:1–10). The Apostle has written a great deal in the two letters to Timothy and in this one now to Titus about the importance of a sound understanding of the Christian faith. There has been much written about sound doctrine and proper order in the church.

Focusing on Titus, Paul writes that he is to speak "the things which become sound doctrine" (2:1). He is to teach and preach about actions that follow "sound doctrine."

As Paul's designated chief pastor for the entire island of Crete, everything Titus said and did would be watched carefully by all the Christians as well as the non-Christians. His words would be repeated and his actions would become the model for all to follow.

This placed a heavy responsibility on Titus, but our load is no lighter. There are those in the office, in the store, on the street, and in the pew across from us who are watching us. As our behavior reflects the love of God, they will be encouraged to share in that love. This is our witness!

Teaching for the Older Men. In the task of leading the church with sound teaching, Paul now gives Titus a list of specific goals for each group within the congregation. His first instructions have to do with the older men (2:2). They are to "be sober, grave, temperate, sound in faith, in charity, in patience."

This bit of instruction was particularly important because frequently a major portion of church leadership is provided by the more mature men. Especially in the first century they would be involved in leadership on the various committees and boards, and they would take the lead in representing the church within the community.

First, Paul has said here these older men were to be sober and clear-minded. Their values were to be mature and free from expressions of excess of any kind.

Second, the older men were to be "grave"—sober, reverent, serious. The reference here is not to someone who has lost the zest and excitement of life. Life at any age is not meant to be dull and drab. Rather, every new day opens up new opportunities, and we are meant to confront them with a holy sense of fun and anticipation. "Joy comes with the morning," and each new day, whether we're thirty or seventy, presents us with a reverent and serious challenge to live creatively for God.

Third, the older men were to be "temperate"—wise, sensible, sane. Experience and wisdom often come with the passing years, and this should enable a person to be more sound in judgment.

Fourth, the older men were to be "sound in faith, in charity, in patience." In one way or another, faith, love, and patience are very much a part of Paul's message to his Christian friends in all the churches. As we grow and mature in the Christian faith, these virtues are to show up more and more in our life-style and to find free expression in our relationships with each other.

Implicit in these instructions, I believe, Paul meant for the older men to assume their role of leadership in the church with a seriousness that was at least equal to their attitude toward their daily work. This then would signal to others on Crete that the gospel of Christ was of greatest importance to these older Christians.

The characteristics Paul has just written about to the older men also apply, especially in our day, to women as well, for their position in the church now is far different and better than what prevailed in Paul's day. Also, what Paul has written here to both the older men and women applies equally as well to all of us regardless of our age. The emphasis here is on holiness (2:2)—an attitude and way of life essential to all Christians.

Teaching for the Older Women.

Holiness means "set-apartness." A person who honestly tries to live a holy life doesn't give in to the temptation to live a "worldly" life-style. Rather, that person recognizes that he or she is set apart by God to *give* and *be* a witness to the Good News.

It is important, though, that we not be misled by the phrase "behaviour as becometh holiness" (2:3). The reference here is not to some form of "super-piety"—an attitude that seems to imply, "I'm better than you." Whether such an attitude is intended or not, it repels people rather than attracts them to the Lord.

In first-century culture, most of the teaching went on in the home. Adult men taught trades to their sons. Adult

Teaching for the Younger Women and Men.

women instructed their daughters in the primary occupation of that time for women—being good wives and mothers (2:4–5).

It would be easy in our day and age to attach feminist significance to these words, but this would be wrong. Paul was instructing Titus in terms of first-century culture. And although family and social patterns are different today for a variety of reasons, the exalted role of wife and mother is even more noble today than it was in the first century. We shouldn't forget either that the role of husband and father is equally noble even though cultural and social conditions are also different than those in Paul's time.

Again, all of the virtues mentioned so far apply to the younger women as well. And we should not get sidetracked by the words in verse 5 that the young women are to be "obedient to their own husbands." This kind of wording should always be viewed in terms of Paul's mutual submission thinking as it was expressed clearly in Ephesians 5.

Then, in verse 6, Paul advises Titus to spend time personally teaching the younger men in the church. Here the Apostle uses the same descriptive word that he did in verse 2. "Sober minded" implies being temperate in behavior. Also I believe Paul wants these younger men to begin to assume a responsible role in the church and in life.

The shift from youth to adulthood is always difficult for young people. Of course, they want to be independent and make their own way. And yet, I have to believe the adult models around them tend to affect the way they move toward assuming the responsibilities of vocation and families and their role as Christians. For this reason, teaching and modeling by more mature persons are very important at this stage of life.

Titus As Model Teacher.   Paul also knew that people of all ages would be watching Titus in his leadership role (2:7–8). And so Titus is urged to always show "a pattern of good works" (2:7). By his actions and life he is to portray a healthy Christ-like style that can be a guide to the Cretan believers. This is indeed a quality of leadership, but since all of us are leaders in God's new society, the Apostle's "pattern of good works" model is meant for us also.

Next, Paul urges Titus as a leader to show or live a pattern of sound and faithful teaching, "In doctrine shewing uncorruptness, gravity, sincerity." The integrity of our understanding and teaching of the Good News is of primary importance.

And finally Titus was to be a leader who had "sound speech" (2:8). Not only were his words and message to have integrity, but the manner in which he presented them was important.

This I believe is an important quality today even as it was in the first century. While, of course, our gifts vary, each of us is to perfect the gifts we have to the best of our ability so that our witness is clear, well-prepared, and understandable. If our speech is "sound," we will avoid the excessive use of Christian jargon and "church talk" in our day-to-day relationships. So many of our expressions take the form of a sort of Christian shorthand—not the least bit understandable to others. And yet if our witness for Christ is to be effective, our words and our meaning must be understood.

Paul now closes out this part of his instructions to Titus by giving him some guidance for first-century slaves who had become Christians. They are urged "to be obedient unto their own masters," to do their work well, and to be faithful (2:9–10).

As in other letters, Paul does not address himself here to the social evil of slavery in first-century society. His concern was that Christians act Christ-like in their daily life. And so the message here is that if the Christian slave was to have any spiritual influence over a master, he or she must serve faithfully and with diligence.

Most certainly this advice has its modern application. If a Christian's work within an office or store is sloppy, if his or her attitude is to get by doing as little as possible—I doubt that anyone would pay much attention to his or her witness. In other words, our Christianity is to show in the quality of our daily work and activities and in our attitudes toward those we work with.

Teaching for Christian Slaves and Workers.

Without pressing too hard, I believe there is a parallel between Titus' mission to "set in order the things that are wanting" in the Cretan church, and our mission as Christians in the late twentieth century. And while it is important that our witness and teaching be focused on sound doctrine, perhaps our most powerful testimony is a good

Our Mission.

example—an authentic pattern of life centered on the one given us by Jesus.

Master, Through Your power I am able to live a life centered in Jesus. You've freed me to obey You and to live above the world's confusion and skewed priorities. AMEN.

WHAT THIS SCRIPTURE MEANS TO ME—Titus 1–2:10

Harry is a tall and virile man who owns the service station near our house. He is always helpful, but he's a *real* friend when George has said for the twelfth time, "Don't you think you ought to take your car to Harry for an oil change?"

I *hate* to take the car to the service station for anything. But Harry is smart enough to know that women also hate to fill the gas tank even though they don't want to spend the extra money at full service pumps. So, he does that for us without charging extra. He knows we will drive ten miles on fumes to experience his courtesy.

Now, Harry has a young helper named Eddie. He's an affable, hardworking young fellow. But some of the persnickety ladies didn't like him because he wore his blond hair down to his shoulders.

"Don't you have a dress code here?" a sour-faced woman asked Harry one day as Eddie was filling up her car at the self-service pump.

There must have been a conspiracy of some kind in the neighborhood because that same day several other picky customers made the same snide remark. Finally, at the end of the day Harry muttered to the kid, "Back you out gettin' a zip!"

The next day both Harry and Eddie were working with clipped-to-the-scalp heads. Their heads were completely shaved. It sure didn't help Harry's looks any, and it made Eddie look too young to be working at the station. Talk about dress codes! And I liked Harry's attitude, too.

In his letter to Titus, Paul described a much more pertinent code, listing those characteristics that are the essence of a committed Christian life-style. Paul was giving Titus the assignment of appointing church leaders in every town in Crete. But he made it clear that these leaders should have certain character qualities. As we saw in our lesson, the behavior code for all of the church leaders was quite strict and demanding.

The aristocratic Greeks of Paul's day understood the importance of a strict behavior code. An aristocrat could not tell a lie—except in love or war. He was never to take advantage of another and was never to cheat anyone. He was to show perfect courage, courtesy to an enemy, and was to be generous as far as his means could be stretched. The aristocrat was to take pride in living up to this severe code and show "a certain magnificence in the conduct of his life." In other words, nobility of birth was to be matched by nobility of conduct. It was this—only with a Christian style and commitment—that Titus was to demand of the Christian leaders he appointed.

Later on in his letter Paul included codes of living for older men, for young men, for older women, and for young women. And as I read Paul's behavior codes for Christians of all ages, and as I reflected again on the pride those Greek aristocrats took in living up to their code, I saw that I can do no less.

Then I remembered the response of Harry and Eddie to the request to a new code, and couldn't help but think, "Boy, wouldn't it create a commotion in my town if we Christians lived up to Paul's code of conduct!"

LESSON 7
TITUS 2:11—3:15

Teachings for Christian Action and a Strong Church

Dear God, Help me to live a sober life, and help me to have a healthy sense of humor—to not take myself or anything about me too seriously. Help me to see things from Your perspective. AMEN.

In Lesson 6 we learned about Paul's plan for establishing order in the Cretan church. First we learned that Titus was to give special care to the selection of leaders (elders) in every city. Then he was to devote himself to the training of those leaders in the great truths of the Christian faith. And finally Titus and those leaders were to be living examples of the faith they taught.

Our lesson now moves on from that point and focuses on the teachings that are essential for Christian growth, as people and as a church. Some of these teachings are about our relationship with God. Others center on our relationships with each other. All of them call us to be a "peculiar people" (2:14)—a special people who are God's very own.

The Grace of God.   Paul concentrates his attention first on the grace of God as he writes, "For the grace of God that bringeth salvation hath appeared to all men, Teaching us that, denying ungodliness and worldly lusts, we should live soberly, righteously, and godly, in this present world" (2:11–12). This is

116

the fundamental truth on which all Christian teaching rests—the grace of God. The knowledge of the grace of God was central in Paul's living, preaching, and writing. And it is this very teaching that Paul wanted as the foundation for the church in Crete.

The early Christians understood that the life, death, and resurrection of Jesus was the ultimate expression of the grace of God. It was through Jesus that sins were forgiven and people were enabled to be in a right relationship with God. They understood that Jesus was the Messiah who had been foretold by their prophets. All of this they saw through Jewish lenses—to them Jesus was exclusively a Jewish Messiah.

This idea presented no problems as long as all the early Christians were Jews. However, as gentiles became Christians, this idea created severe complications. To many of the early church leaders the natural order of things seemed to be for these gentiles to become Jews first—the males were to be circumcised and everyone was to follow the Jewish Law. Then they could be baptized and admitted into the Christian church.

But Paul understood God's grace in a different and more personal way. He was a Jew, a Pharisee, and in his early days he had been a violent persecutor of Christians. In fact, it was his religious zeal that had him on his way to Damascus to arrest Christians when he first met Christ. Yet the Apostle knew that for all of his faithfulness and zeal he had never experienced the love and grace of God until that dramatic meeting. It was then that he realized that being accepted by God had nothing to do with following the Law. Rather, acceptance was by God's grace through Jesus Christ. And furthermore, that grace was for "all men," everyone in the world irrespective of race, and not just for the Jews.

It was this knowledge that led Paul to accept his assignment to be the apostle to the gentiles—a revolutionary idea to one of his race and rank. And so he traveled extensively to teach that God's grace was for everybody—a person did not have to become a Jew before becoming a Christian.

So we see that one of the early Christian struggles was this narrow view of God's grace, which limited it racially and philosophically as well as religiously. Although Paul had won his point at the Jerusalem Council that God's grace was open to gentiles who received Christ, and that they didn't have to meet any other conditions, the history of the Christian church has often been marred by those who still want to "put God's grace in a box."

Today, as never before, our world is compressed in time and size. Through television especially our world view and understanding include cultures and political systems vastly different from our own. The church, the Body of Christ, is "alive and well" and even flourishing under conditions far different from any we understand and are comfortable with.

It is as important today as it was in the first century that we western Christians not limit God's grace and expression to our ideologies. Instead, we will do well to remember Paul's words—that the grace of God makes salvation available to everyone irrespective of political and social boundaries.

Our Response to God's Grace.

God's gracious provision of life through Christ calls for a response from people in all time. It demands a choice. We can choose to accept it and discover the freedom and fulfillment it brings, or we can ignore and reject it and continue living with fear and hopelessness—alienated from God.

But as Paul continues his instruction here, he makes it clear that the call of grace is to righteous living (2:12). Throughout all of his writings Paul insists that righteous living does not mean following a given set of rules. Rather, it is by living in obedience to the words Jesus spoke when He responded to the question, "Which is the first commandment of all? And Jesus answered him, The first of all the commandments is, Hear, O Israel; the Lord our God is one Lord: And thou shalt love the Lord thy God with all thy heart, and with all thy soul, and with all thy mind, and with all thy strength: this is the first commandment. And the second is like, namely this, Thou shalt love thy neighbour as thyself. There is none other commandment greater than these" (Mark 12:28–31). This is the Christian response to God's grace.

The New Testament gives us many images and pictures to help us understand more fully what Jesus meant by this statement. For example, the writer of the first letter to John asks how a person can love God whom he or she hasn't seen if that person does not love his or her brother (1 John 4:20). The answer comes through clearly in the next verse,

"And this commandment have we from him, That he who loveth God love his brother also." For us that seems to mean that we show our love for God by loving our neighbors in the world.

When Jesus told the remarkable story about the Good Samaritan, He elaborated on the question, "Who is my neighbor?" (Luke 10:29–37). This story clearly identifies our neighbor as anyone who has a need. Geographical proximity, racial similarity, or creedal agreement does not determine who our neighbor is.

Now, as we piece this together, the picture comes clear. For Jesus, living the Christian life is to love God with our whole being and to love our neighbors in the world as much as we love and care for ourselves. This is the same idea that Paul calls righteousness, and it is our call by the grace of God. I know this is rather a lengthy discussion of a very few words in this part of Paul's letter to Titus, but God's grace is at the foundation of everything we call Christian, and I believe our "neighbors" today are anxious to see a practical demonstration of that grace in your life and mine.

Hope for the Future.

Paul turns his attention next to a subject that has been of utmost importance to Christians since Jesus left this earth from the slopes of the Mount of Olives. Here he refers to "that blessed hope, and the glorious appearing of the great God and our Saviour Jesus Christ; Who gave himself for us, that he might redeem us from all iniquity" (2:13–14). Paul knew that this great affirmation was important to the vigor of the Cretan Christians.

But to affirm the death and resurrection of Jesus and to live in anticipation of His Second Coming doesn't mean we should reject our life in this present world. I have known those, as I'm sure you have, who professed to want no part of what is happening now in this life and were completely preoccupied with the next world. I've heard them say, "There is no hope for this world. We can only wait for the next. Christ is coming soon."

But affirming the resurrection of Jesus and waiting expectantly for the appearing of Christ is to recognize that God has powerfully blessed *this* world! Belief in the resurrection affirms that Christ was raised from the dead in *this* world! We wait for the Second Coming of Christ because it's a time when God will restore order and harmony in *this*

To the left is a view along the Via Sacra in Ephesus and to the right is the monument to Caesar Augustus in the agora at Ephesus.

world. And in affirming these marvelous truths we indicate that our hope is in *this* world. Such being the case, our task is to work for the coming of God's kingdom now—in *this* world.

A Special People.   The Christian community—the church—Paul writes is made up of "peculiar"—special—people who are anxious to live for God. Because of the wording of the King James text there have been those who by dress and mannerisms seemed to feel there was virtue in being odd. But I don't believe that is what is meant here.

It is true, though, that the Christian is special—different. But the difference is found in our worldview and value system. Christians are regular people with regular

jobs who live regular lives. Some are quite poor while others are wealthy. Some are highly educated and others haven't been to school. But all are special because of their upside-down view of success. Success for the Christian is not measured by how much we receive, but by how much we give. And Christians take seriously the words of Jesus, "Whosoever of you will be the chiefest, shall be servant of all" (Mark 10:44).

When, as Christians, we see ourselves as "special" people, we acknowledge that the organizing principle of our lives is larger than ourselves—it reaches out to the whole world. And our greatest desire is to follow the teachings of our Lord and live for Him in the world of here and now.

We move now into the closing part of this remarkable little letter with some very practical advice—be good cit-

Good Citizenship.

izens, "Be subject to principalities and powers, to obey magistrates" (3:1). Now, as we read earlier, the people of Crete were not particularly known for their good moral behavior. They were an unruly and lawless people who were not very good citizens.

In a setting like this a Christian citizen with the qualities of life Paul mentions here (3:1–2) would stand out like a sore thumb. Paul writes that a Christian citizen obeys the law and is involved in the life of his or her community, doesn't put down or talk against other people, isn't a troublemaker, and is always gentle and polite. It doesn't take a whole lot of imagination to picture the difference a group of citizens like that would have made in first-century Crete. But that is precisely why these instructions were important! Their witness and active participation in community affairs could not help but be a Christ-like influence on everything that went on. And while it isn't likely that any of our towns have bad reputations like those Cretan cities, Christian citizens who fit Paul's description here will make a big difference anywhere. I believe very strongly that making a difference in the world around us is our Christian calling.

"Ready to Every Good Work."

Before we leave this first verse of Chapter 3, however, we need to look closely at six of Paul's most important words, "Be ready to every good work." Here is the "why" to Paul's teaching so far. The Christian is to be prepared *to do good* at every opportunity. It is this that gives our faith an outward expression. If we say that the love of Christ has changed us, then our actions should prove it.

The great reformer, Martin Luther, was a keen student of Paul's writings, but in his zeal to correct the works-oriented approach of the medieval church he somehow missed or underplayed this part of the Apostle's teachings. His Reformation battle cry was "The just shall live by faith" (Rom. 1:17). The idea that salvation is a gift of God through faith had been a sadly neglected teaching.

But faith was never supposed to be set in opposition to our action-oriented response to God's grace. In fact, it is only by faith that we can give ourselves so completely to the work that is ours to do. It is by faith that we give ourselves to feeding the hungry, fighting disease, or working for peace and equality.

As Christians and as members of the church we are

called to be active in our community and in the world, "ready to do every good work" in response to our faith in Christ.

In verse 2, as we have seen, Paul spelled out clearly those qualities that make a good Christian citizen. Now, because of the Apostle's keen understanding of people, he gives Titus a needed reminder in verse 3—they were not to become proud of their Christian accomplishments or to be judgmental. After all, they once "were sometimes foolish, disobedient, deceived, serving divers lusts and pleasures, living in malice and envy, hateful, and hating one another."

A Needed Reminder.

This reminder is as important to us as it was to the Cretan Christians. We are what we are only because of God's grace. At best our "piety" falls far short in terms of both intent and actions when set alongside the teachings of Jesus. When we are tempted to be judgmental of others, we would do well to look at Paul's "reminder list" in verse 3 and ask, "Are we ever disobedient? Do we ever give in to any desire that detracts from being at our best for God? Do we ever have feelings of bitterness and envy over someone else's success? Are we ever hateful in the way we talk about someone else—do we put them down in a sarcastic way? Are we ever guilty of expressing our hate for someone by ignoring them?"

We are also reminded here of Jesus' well-chosen words to His disciples when He told them they should first examine their own lives before even thinking about being critical of someone else (Luke 6:42). The true awareness of what and where we are in Christ by His grace will cut off critical and judgmental attitudes.

The reminder continues. While we were once guilty of the sinfulness described in verse 3, "But after that the kindness and love of God our Saviour toward man appeared, Not by works of righteousness which we have done, but according to his mercy, he saved us, by the washing of regeneration, and renewing of the Holy Ghost: Which he shed on us abundantly through Jesus Christ our Saviour" (3:4–7).

This impassioned reminder tells us that our salvation— our life in Christ and all the joy and fulfillment it brings to us—is a gift of God. It is a gift made possible through the death and resurrection of Jesus and the renewing of the Holy Spirit and is far more than an intellectual under-

123

standing. Rather, it is a passionate awareness that explodes from the depths of our hearts—our inner beings—that first turns us to a new direction and then keeps us on course in spite of our human frailties. This is God's grace at work in your heart and mine. And it is by this grace that we have our "hope of eternal life" (3:7).

Paul is reminding us here that God's grace not only helps us find meaning in our present life on this earth as we know it, but it gives us hope and assurance for the future. The findings of anthropologists have long suggested that most of the people of this world, irrespective of their religion, have some belief that life goes on in the "hereafter." For the Christian that belief is firm. We not only have promises like this one and others in God's Word, but there is that deep and mysterious inner assurance of the promise of the Resurrection.

A Further Reminder "to Maintain Good Works."

In the final teaching section of this letter (3:8–11) Paul sums up what he has just been saying by adding, "I will that thou affirm *constantly*, that they which have believed in God might be careful to maintain good works. These things are good and profitable unto men" (3:8, italics mine).

It seems to me that Paul's repeated emphasis calls for us to take a closer look at our role in doing "good works." His use of the word "constantly" implies continued and aggressive action. We get the picture here that there is no way we can be spectators in God's arena—we are participants in the action, aggressively involved in God's work in the world.

At the same time, though, we must remain "constantly" aware that it is God at work in and through us that makes it possible for us to act in His behalf. The Apostle himself in another letter explains and clarifies the balance here, "...work out your own salvation with fear and trembling. For it is God which worketh in you both to *will and to do* of his good pleasure" (Phil. 2:12–13, italics mine).

Paul next goes on with his "maintenance" instructions. To be continually involved in God's work the Christian is to avoid getting sidetracked by senseless arguments and debates—fine points of Jewish Law—because "they are unprofitable and vain [useless]" (3:9). Paul's warning is clear even as it has been in other letters. He is responding to those Greeks who loved to argue fine points for the sake of parading their "knowledge," and to those Jews who were stirring up strife and trouble by their insistence on following Jewish tradition and Law. The Apostle's response is straight to the point—all of this is useless!

Again, as we look around at Christian behavior today and at the work of the church, the application is painfully clear. The "good works" of Christians and the church in the world are so often subjected to a destructive influence by contentious—though possibly at times sincere—people who are critical of any who disagree with them and who may even want to exclude them from Christian fellowship. Quibbling over minor and non-critical points of difference is useless.

On the other hand, there may be those in the church who are causing strife and division with heretical ideas that are entirely contrary to Scripture and the traditions of the church. Such persons are usually convinced that they and they alone are the only custodians of the truth and *everyone* else is wrong. Paul says these people are to be properly confronted and then if they persist, they are to be excluded from the fellowship.

The underlying emphasis of Paul's teaching here, I believe, is that truth is a uniting and cohesive agent among Christians. It is not intended to be divisive.

Personal Greetings and a Final Reminder.

Paul now draws this letter to a close in his usual fashion. He mentions four people—Artemas, Tychicus, Zenas, and Apollos. Only two of these names are familiar to us because of their mention elsewhere. Tychicus, of course, was a confidante and coworker of Paul. He delivered the letters addressed to the Ephesian and Colossian churches, and on at least one occasion served the church at Ephesus during Timothy's absence.

Apollos is mentioned in both Acts and 1 Corinthians. He was widely known throughout the Christian community as a gifted teacher and preacher.

Among these closing greetings we catch something of Paul's personal feelings and concerns. First, he mentions his strong desire for a personal visit with Titus. Here and in his other letters we sense the Apostle's strong attachment to certain of his special friends and fellow-workers.

Then in verse 13 Paul asks Titus to be helpful to Zenas and Apollos in their travels. The Apostle wants to make certain that their needs are met insofar as it is possible.

Both of these personal references might on the surface

seem too small to mention. But I think on even such seemingly minor matters as these we can learn from Paul as he demonstrates in so many ways how people are important to him. The Christian faith isn't lived in isolation. Paul needed his friends and fellow-workers. He needed their support, and in turn he was particularly sensitive in showing caring concern for them.

I think Paul's example is particularly important for us. Having friends is one of God's special gifts—and being a friend is one of our greatest gifts. A writer not known to me captured the importance of friends with these words, "Jesus' home was the road along which he walked with his friends in search of new friends."

Again and again in this short letter the Apostle has stressed the importance of good works—of doing good as an outward witness of the Christian faith. But now, one last time, he returns to that theme: "maintain good works" (3:14). He feels so strongly about the importance of doing good that he repeats the refrain one more time. In doing so we feel his urgency. Let's face it, our neighbors next door and across the world will know we're Christians by our acts.

Throughout the letter Paul has emphasized the theme of grace. And now he closes with "Grace be with you all. Amen."

Paul's letter to Titus is short—three chapters with a total of only forty-six verses. It was written to a first-century Christian leader that we don't know much about, and this leader was at the time of writing the chief pastor or overseer of the Christians on the island of Crete. And we know little about them except what comes through in the wording of this letter.

It would be easy to miss the importance of this letter. And yet Paul's instruction on church organization and the qualities of leadership are invaluable. Then, too, his practical instructions on living the Christian life, his stress on God's grace coupled with his repeated emphasis on "good works" as an evidence of that grace lays before us a challenge for Christian life and mission today. Somehow it seems that the problems and needs of those first-century Christians on that obscure island of Crete have their parallels in our Christian community today.

Once again, we learn much from Paul!

Father, Help me "to maintain the good works" You've prepared for
me to perform. AMEN.

LESSON SEVEN

WHAT THIS SCRIPTURE MEANS TO ME—Titus 2:11–3:15

Through the years, George and I have entertained church and school groups, women's organizations and civic clubs with our folk singing and his guitar. One particular evening we were not only running late getting to the meeting, but we had not planned our program completely. Furthermore, we had not picked up the sitter. The day had been frustratingly full, and I had not yet prepared the girls' supper.

As we were wildly trying to do everything at one time, something snapped, and I ran screaming down the hall of our small house, "I cannot stand it! This is too much!" Throwing myself on our bed for a good cry, I was suddenly aware that someone had walked silently into the room. It was seven-year-old Polly.

I jerked up into a sitting position, instantly ashamed.

"Oh, Polly, I'm so sorry. That was no way for a mother to behave," and I hugged her hard.

"That's all right," she replied, leaning against me, "I get tired, too."

Then I cried a little more from the joy of that instant forgiveness and understanding. The scene I've just described came to mind when I read this Scripture lesson. So often we're foolish and disobedient. We become critical and hateful—thinking and saying things that are hurtful and damaging to or about someone. But then when we come to ourselves and ask forgiveness we sense the forgiving presence and love of God.

God's grace is so available and regenerative that it is beyond our ability to comprehend it. When Polly said, "That's all right. I get tired, too," I got a whole new understanding of what it means to receive the offer of forgiveness. She was a child, but she understood the need to be generous with other people's frustrations, and anger and foibles.

My father tells the story of a man who died after living a fruitless and evil life in a certain small community. As the local ministers approached his funeral service, they couldn't come up with one good thing to say about the old fellow. Finally, someone suggested they consult with Mrs. Smith, who was widely known for her generous spirit.

"Have you seen any good in this man?" they asked. "Can you think of one good thing we can say about him?"

"Well," she said after a long pause, "he had the prettiest teeth of anybody in town." Mrs. Smith was the epitome of a gentle and generous spirit.

I wonder if our strongest witness to the love and grace of God is in being forgiving and gentle and courteous to the people in our lives—the clerk at the grocery checkout counter, the postman, the paper boy, the garbage man, the man who takes care of our car at the service station. Somehow, I strongly suspect this speaks much louder than any theological discussion or the quoting of Scripture!

LESSON 8
PHILEMON

Daily Christian Living

God, Open my eyes to see You in my daily living; You've re-deemed even the ordinary and mundane. Sensitize me to Your quickening touch. AMEN.

This letter of Paul to Philemon is the most personal letter in the New Testament, and it is the only private letter of Paul that we have. It is a piece of intimate correspondence from Paul to one of his closest friends, but we can also tell from the wording that the Apostle not only loved Philemon as a close friend; he also had a high regard for his commitment to Jesus Christ.

Unlike Paul's other letters, his primary purpose in writing this time was not to interpret the faith or to specifically define Christian behavior. Rather, this letter emphasizes daily Christian living in a most practical way. It shows us how faith in Jesus Christ affects the everyday life of those who are committed to Him.

Philemon is a behind-the-scenes letter that captures the personhood of Paul in a warm and intimate way. His passionate concern for other people—in this case for Onesimus the slave—is portrayed more vividly here than anywhere else.

A thoughtful look at Paul's letters indicates the high

We Learn about Paul.

129

value he placed on friendship. This idea comes into much bolder relief as we read this letter and sense the great respect and love the Apostle had for this particular friend. In verses 8 and 9 we see that Paul could evidently have been much more insistent in the request he was making of his friend. While he apparently felt he had the right to make demands, he didn't make any. Instead, he made his request and left the decision up to his friend.

We also find in this bit of correspondence a colorful portrayal of Paul's sensitivity to people as human beings. Paul's critics over the centuries have condemned him for his apparent silence on the subject of the social evil of slavery, but I don't believe they've seen him in the proper light.

Slaves in the first-century Roman world had no rights. Their masters held absolute authority over them. In that brutal and repressive society a slave's life was of no consequence. Had the handful of Christians in the first century done anything to inspire the revolt of the 60,000,000 slaves in the Empire, the brutal reprisals might have exploded into a bloodbath that could have resulted in the extermination of slave and Christian alike.

And yet as the saga of this short letter unravels, we see a Paul whose words and actions clearly interpret his view of slavery. Even with the hindsight of almost 2,000 years of history, I think we still have to say that Paul's insistence on proper Christian behavior within the structure and mores of the time was best. For him "There is neither Greek nor Jew, circumcision nor uncircumcision, Barbarian, Scythian, *bond nor free*: but Christ is all, and in all" (Col. 3:11, italics mine).

Then, I found something else in this letter that gave me new insights into Paul as a person. For me, at least, this letter gives me a view of his sense of humor. For example in verse 11 Paul seems to resort to some punning. The meaning of the Greek name Onesimus, Philemon's runaway slave, was "profitable." With this in mind, the Apostle's play on words takes on a tongue-in-cheek sound—in the past, Onesimus (the profitable one) had been useless or "unprofitable" to Philemon. But now, because of his conversion and his time with Paul, Onesimus measured up to his name and was "profitable" and useful.

The lighthearted touch seems to continue when Paul mentions that in making his important request of Philemon in this letter he has not made an issue of Philemon's great debt toward him. There is none of this, "I scratched your back once, now you scratch mine" routine. And the Apostle continues in verse 21 to say that he hadn't applied pressure to get a favorable answer to his request because he just knew that his good friend would give him far more than what he asked for.

And finally, in verse 9, Paul exhibits a lighthearted approach when he refers to himself as "Paul the aged." It takes a good sense of humor to see yourself as "aged" and as a "prisoner" and then go on to write that if Onesimus owes Philemon anything it is to be charged "on mine account" (1:18).

I emphasize these very warm and human traits of Paul because for far too long he has been pictured as a rather stern and formidable person. Instead, as we've seen in our studies, he is a caring, compassionate human being with the ability to use puns and to see the lighthearted side of life.

We Learn about Philemon.

As we read this letter, we also learn a great deal about Philemon, the person to whom it is addressed. In fact, what little we know about him comes entirely from this short letter.

It seems apparent that Philemon was an active layperson in the Lycus Valley churches. While he is generally believed to have been located in Colossae, we do know there were two other related Christian communities close by in Laodicea and Hieropolis. It has also been speculated by some interpreters that Philemon actually lived in Laodicea, but whichever place, it is likely that his influence was felt in all three congregations.

We don't know just how this close friendship developed between Paul and Philemon. Some students of the Apostle believe that he never visited the Lycus Valley churches. Others believe it is possible that he did, and if this was the case, that he may have stayed in Philemon's home. If true, this would, of course, be one answer to the friendship question.

We also gather from Paul's wording in this letter that Philemon's faith in Christ deeply affected his daily life. This comes through in the way Paul expected Philemon to receive Onesimus on his return. It was common practice for runaway slaves to receive brutal treatment from their masters if they were apprehended. But Paul anticipated a completely different and merciful reaction from his friend. We get the feeling that he knew Philemon so well that Paul was certain of his "Christian" response.

We Learn about Daily Christian Living.

A reading of this remarkable little letter gives us important insight into how our Christian faith is to influence our actions in the give-and-take of daily life. Paul's emphasis on acting out our faith—not just talking about our faith—comes through clearly in his correspondence with his friend.

More about the Letter.

Before we move in for a closer look at this intimate bit of correspondence, I want to make a few more generalized observations about it and its place in our New Testament. While Philemon is generally positioned with Timothy and Titus, it isn't technically one of the "Pastoral Epistles." Both of the Timothy letters and the Titus letter came much later than Philemon.

However, we are studying Philemon now because it follows the Timothy and Titus letters. It is placed where it is because it is the shortest of Paul's letters. There has also been considerable speculation over the centuries as to why this short, personal letter was included in our New Testament since it includes no major theological statements, even though we do get valuable insights into practical Christian living.

It is possible, however, that tradition gives us some insight into the reason we have this valuable little letter in our New Testament. According to early church tradition the earliest collection of Paul's letters was brought together in Ephesus around the end of the first century or the begining of the second. It is believed by many that the bishop of the Ephesian church at that time was this same Onesimus who was the runaway slave of the letter to Philemon.

Near the beginning of the second century, Ignatius, an early church father and martyr, wrote a lengthy letter to the church in Ephesus in which he gave high praise to their bishop. An excerpt from this ancient letter reads, "I received the welcome of your congregation in the presence of Onesimus, your bishop in this world, a man whose love is beyond words. My prayer is that you should love him in the spirit of Jesus Christ and all be like him. Blessed is he who let you have such a bishop."

There are, of course, gaps in the story, and there is much that we don't know. But it is not unreasonable to speculate and ask ourselves, "In response to this short letter that we are studying now, did Philemon accept his runaway slave back as a fellow Christian and then give him his freedom? And, based on his relationship with Paul in Rome, did Onesimus then grow and mature in the Christian faith and indeed become *this* bishop, or overseer, who was the traditional bishop of Ephesus and the one Ignatius referred to in his letter?"

If, indeed, Onesimus, Philemon's runaway slave, was the bishop of Ephesus early in the second century at the time Paul's letters were being collected for safekeeping and further use, it wouldn't be the least bit surprising that he insisted that Paul's very personal letter, written in his behalf, to his former master Philemon, be preserved with the rest of the Apostle's writings. There is no way we can know for sure, but such a scenario is well within the realm of possibility with God!

The Opening of the Letter.

From the information given in the opening verses of the letter (1–3), we get a picture of the setting in which it was written. Paul writes that he is "a prisoner of Jesus Christ." This letter is generally dated by most scholars as early in Paul's prison period in Rome.

Verse 1 also identifies Timothy as the co-author of the letter. This means the letter was likely written during the time Timothy was visiting Paul while he was under house arrest as mentioned in Acts 28. In line with his usual custom, Paul immediately identifies the person to whom he is writing, "Philemon our dearly beloved, and fellowlabourer."

The Apostle then goes on in verse 2 to write that the letter is also for "our beloved Apphia, and Archippus our fellowsoldier, and to the church in thy house." Now, these two people are not identified further; however, speculation has it that Apphia was Philemon's wife and Archippus was his son. If not, they may have been a couple in the church who were close friends of both Paul and Philemon. And in keeping with the pattern of the time, they were all involved and active in a house church, "The church in thy house." You will remember that early in the life of the church there were no church buildings—the Christians usually met in someone's home for study and worship.

All of this tells us that while this is a personal letter to Philemon, Paul intended for it to be shared with the whole church. I suspect Paul thought that everyone would benefit from hearing what he had written and then from seeing the example that he knew Philemon would show in his treatment of the returning Onesimus. Then, too, we see Paul's humorous side exposed in his suggestion that what he had written be read aloud—it wasn't likely Philemon would say "no" to his request when all of the other Christians knew what Paul was asking.

Paul's Feelings for Philemon.

Next, in verses 4–7, Paul expresses his appreciation for Philemon's love and faith as it was acted out in his day-to-day life. The reference to "thy love and faith, which thou hast toward the Lord Jesus, and toward all the saints" especially attracted my attention. We learn from this that Philemon's Christian life was well balanced between devotion and service. He was faithful in his devotional life of prayer and worship, but he expressed his love and devotion through his compassion and service toward others. The picture we get here is that Paul knew Philemon acted out his faith in Christ in his service to his brothers and sisters in the Lord. It would have been out of character for Philemon to ever say to anyone, "I'm sorry, I'm too busy to help you now because I'm serving God."

From Paul's words in these four verses we get a vivid picture of Philemon's devotion to God and his fellow Christians. He, in fact, gives us a model for our own Christian pilgrimage—a model of Christian devotion to the Lord and to the church and a model of loving compassion for our brothers and sisters in Christ. Paul's meaning in verse 7 is obscured somewhat by our King James text. He is telling Philemon that the Christians around him are refreshed and encouraged by his faith and actions. This is our mission—to refresh and encourage the people we work and worship with in our churches every Sunday.

Paul Asks a Favor.

We come now to the very heart and purpose of this letter (1:8–9). Paul has a great favor to ask of his dear friend. And here, as I mentioned earlier, we get a glimpse of Paul's sense of humor as he prepares Philemon for the request.

Yes, Paul says, because of his status as the apostle to the gentiles—by virtue of his role as a leader in the church—he could demand a favorable response to the favor he is about to ask. But "for love's sake" he is merely asking as a friend.

It is important that we understand that Paul wasn't resorting to flattery to get what he wanted. He was not attempting to manipulate his friend for the desired results. I just have to think that he knew before asking that Phile-

Paul's letter to Philemon is one of his most personal. Philemon was a leading Christian in the Lycus Valley. Clustered within a few miles of each other were three groups of Christians at Colossae (Philemon's home), Laodicea, and Hierapolis. Pictured here is a valley seen near the ancient site of Colossae.

mon's response would be favorable and that he knew Philemon knew that as well. If this were not the case, I don't think Paul would have put his friend on the spot publicly. He was much too gentle and loving for that.

In what appears to be a bit of byplay here we get further insight into the heart of Paul. He knows his friend so well that he is sure his request—his favor—will be granted. But he's gentle and tactful and even a bit lighthearted in his approach. There is no "bull in the china shop" Paul at work here. There is no "means justifying the ends" philosophy. Paul was not being a humorless legalist by demanding what was due him. Instead, we see "Paul the aged" and a "prisoner" in good humor asking a favor of a friend.

The Favor. Paul now makes his appeal, "I rather beseech thee *for my son* Onesimus, whom I have begotten in my bonds" (1:10, italics mine). Paul is telling Philemon that his runaway slave is now "my son" because he found Christ in the Apostle's prison cell. In verse 12 Paul makes it clear that he is sending Onesimus home in anticipation of his being well received. And in verse 11, the Apostle reminds Philemon that his slave hasn't been of much use to him up to now, but as a Christian, he will be useful. Onesimus was a new man in Christ. His attitudes and his actions were different. And Paul knew that to be a fact because Onesimus had been so helpful to him in his prison confinement.

Paul's intercession for his friend Onesimus is a moving account of the Apostle's love for his young friend whom he hopes will be well received in spite of his earlier misbehavior. And then Paul adds in verse 13 that he would have liked very much to have kept Onesimus with him so that he could have been of help to Paul in the discomfort of his confinement. But then he hurries to add in verse 14 that he wouldn't have done that without Philemon's consent.

I suspect also that in sending Onesimus back to the Lycus Valley to Philemon's home, Paul was emphasizing the importance of righting the wrong that had been committed in the escape. Onesimus had sinned against his master, and that sin had to be made right.

At the same time, Paul may have been laying a hint here that he hoped Philemon would catch. If after returning home, Onesimus was given his freedom by Philemon, he could return to Rome and continue to help Paul endure his confinement. But, obviously, this was a decision that only Philemon could make.

While verses 15 and 16 are specifically written about Onesimus, they give a perfect picture of what happens when a person is captured by the Good News of a new life in Christ. Paul admits to Philemon that while his slave had left "for a season"—for a while—that he was coming back as more than a slave. He was coming back forever, but now as a brother in the Lord. After leaving, Onesimus was an outlaw that could have been hunted down and killed. But on returning, he was a brother to be received the same way Philemon would have welcomed Paul.

In this movement from runaway slave to a returned brother in Christ, we get a picture of what happens to a person who has been converted and returned to a right relationship with God. In a sense we are all runaways, but then at some point through God's grace we come back home. We had "separated for a season," but then God received us back forever. And now we are Onesimus—useful—for the Lord's service.

When Philemon received Onesimus back into his household, he received more than a runaway slave—he got his servant back, but he also received a Christian brother. The Apostle worded it this way after asking Philemon to receive Onesimus forever, "Not now as a servant, but above a servant, a brother beloved, specially to me, but how much more unto thee...?"

This part of our story reminds me of someone else who "came home." His name was John, an acquaintance of mine from college. John grew up in a suburban church and was active in Sunday school, the youth choir, and the youth athletic programs. Then in his later high school years he taught a Sunday school class and coached a children's softball team.

When John left home for college, he transferred to a church in the college community and became active. That's where I met him. And while he was in college, he met a beautiful Christian girl with whom he fell in love and eventually married.

After John graduated from college, he and Betty moved to his hometown where he found a very good job. It wasn't long, though, before John stopped going to

Onesimus Is Now a Brother.

church. He was so involved in getting ahead that he frequently worked Sundays. At the same time the social pressure was building up as he struggled to "keep up" with the other young executives in the community.

Then John started to drink quite heavily, and he and Betty drifted apart until she couldn't take it any more and moved out. Betty told John that she loved him and always would, but she wouldn't move back until he got straightened out.

The shock of Betty's leaving caused John to take a hard look at his life. And he came to me one afternoon asking for help. I got him into a program for problem drinkers, and we spent hours together just talking. It wasn't long until John was back and active in the church, and after a few months he asked Betty to move back home again. She did, and together the two of them started to put their marriage back together again.

It was then that their pastor did a most unusual but wise thing. One Sunday morning he preached a sermon on Onesimus and used John as a modern day example. "John," he said, "you left us for a while. You had to see if you could make it on your own. While you were away, we lost someone very special to us. When you returned, we felt that we had you back forever, as a servant of the Lord and as a dear Christian brother. Welcome home, John!"

What a beautiful expression of Christian love! That is the way Paul wanted Philemon to treat his runaway slave. And, somehow, Paul knew that's exactly what he would do.

Repetition for Emphasis. When any of us wants to be sure to get a point across, we sometimes resort to repeating ourselves for emphasis. That's what I think Paul was doing in verse 17 when he wrote, "If thou count me therefore a partner, receive him [Onesimus] as myself." In other words, the Apostle is asking Philemon to treat Onesimus just as he would if Paul himself had arrived. And Paul knew that Philemon regarded him not only as a partner and fellow-worker in the Lord, but as one of his closest friends.

Paul's words here reminded me of an incident that happened not long ago. My good friend Tommy lives in Austin, Texas. One day Tommy called me up in Northeast Texas to ask if I had a spare bedroom where I could entertain for just one night a special friend of his who had been his roommate in college. It seems that Ben and his wife were traveling to northern Alabama to spend Christmas with their parents. I live about halfway between Austin and their final destination.

While I had met Ben and his wife just once, I knew that if Tommy vouched for them, they had to be all right. So I agreed that they could spend the night at my house. In a sense, I received Ben and his wife into my home as I would have received my good friend Tommy.

Hospitality is an important Christian virtue. And as I have reflected further on the Onesimus and the Ben story, I am reminded of Jesus' words which get the point across that if "ye do it unto the least of these, ye do it unto me."

An Offer to Pay Up.

Next, Paul wants to make sure that nothing will stand in the way of Philemon's open acceptance of Onesimus, so he offers to pay any debt his runaway slave may have caused. He promises to pay for anything Onesimus may have taken with him when he ran away. In all probability, Onesimus had absconded with a considerable sum in order for him to make his way the long distance from Colossae to Rome.

As I mentioned in the introductory part of this lesson, we once again catch a little of Paul's humor here. Let's face it, as a prisoner of Rome, Paul was probably in pretty dire financial straits himself. But he emphasizes his promise by calling Philemon's attention to the fact that he has not dictated this letter but has written it himself. His promise to pay is in his own handwriting. Then, with what had to be a twinkle in his eye, the Apostle added that he would do this even though Philemon already owed him a favor. In other words, Paul is saying, "I'll pay you anything Onesimus owes you, even though you already owe me a big favor." I'm convinced Paul isn't being manipulative here, but humorous and tactful, and he's pretty sure Philemon will interpret his offer in the spirit in which it was made.

Paul's Confidence.

I believe that in verses 20 and 21 Paul pays Philemon the highest compliment anyone can pay a friend. The Apostle has complete confidence in his friend. This theme has been prevalent throughout the letter, but now he adds, "Having confidence in thy obedience"—that you will do what I ask— "I wrote unto thee, knowing that thou wilt also do more than I say." There was never a question in Paul's mind as to how his friend would respond.

To be that kind of friend—one that can be counted on under all circumstances—is a powerful witness to the unconditional love of God. And to have a friend that we know we can count on under all circumstances is a gift to be nurtured and treasured. Paul and Philemon model for us here one of the greatest of Christian virtues.

Closing Comments and Benediction.

As Paul moves now to bring his letter to a close, we see his spirit of optimism at its best. Even though he is in prison, he hopes to be released and to make a visit to Philemon's home in Colossae (1:22). Irrespective of present circumstances, Paul's hope is in God.

We see nothing of gloom or doom in Paul's attitude. His faith was firm. There's a lesson for us here that deserves attention. We find it easy to have faith and hope when

Another scene that was likely familiar to Philemon and to his slave Onesimus. This is a view of the theater ruins at Laodicea.

140

things are going smoothly. But the true test comes in our hard times—times when the future is obscured and trouble is piled high on all sides. It is for such moments that the Apostle's words to his friends in Philippi take on new meaning, "I have learned in whatsoever state I am, therewith to be content" (Phil. 4:11). And it is then that the full force of our concentration should focus on Paul's grand affirmation, "I can do all things through Christ which strengtheneth me" (Phil. 4:13).

Paul next includes the greetings of those who are with him. He mentions Epaphras, whom he identifies here as a fellowprisoner in Christ Jesus and whom he referred to earlier as a "dear fellowservant" and a "faithful minister of Christ" (Col. 1:7). Then he mentions Aristarchus from Macedonia who had traveled with him (Acts 19:29), and Demas, whom Paul had also mentioned in his letter to the Colossians (4:14). And included in the list are Marcus (Mark) and Lucas (Luke) who are quite likely the Gospel writers. All of these men were important to Paul as "fellowlabourers."

And, finally, come the familiar words of benediction, "The grace of our Lord Jesus Christ be with your spirit. Amen." The theme of grace runs through all of Paul's writings. And well it might, for it was grace that transformed his life when he met the Savior on the Damascus road, and it was grace that motivated his thoughts and actions and writings as he moved across the Roman world as a missionary of the Good News.

In Conclusion.

In this, the shortest and most personal of Paul's letters, we find an intensely practical and timely message for our times as we move from the twentieth century toward the twenty-first. There are three central characters who are a part of the action and the message.

It is likely that Paul and Philemon first became friends and Christian brothers in Ephesus, a hundred or so miles west of Colossae. In them we see God at work in the lives of two committed Christians who clearly understood that faith in Christ involved more than a profession—it involved action in response to their profession in the living of their daily lives, including their relationships with each other and their fellow Christians.

The third character, of course, is the runaway slave, Onesimus, who somehow came in contact with Paul in his prison confinement and was converted to faith in Jesus Christ. Here we see an outlaw changed by God's grace and transformed into a Christian brother. These three unlikely men—Paul, a highly educated Pharisee turned missionary; Philemon, a wealthy gentile merchant in the Lycus Valley in the Roman province of Asia; and Onesimus, a runaway slave with no personal rights—come together to give us a picture of practical Christianity at work in the first-century church and in the lives of those early Christians in bringing about personal commitment and social change. Here we see in living color that *all* Christians are equal as brothers and sisters and are to be accepted in love.

Lord God, Help me to love and accept people who are different from me. Help me to see them as You do. AMEN.

WHAT THIS SCRIPTURE MEANS TO ME—Philemon

I called her Aunt Sal until I started school, and then I had to use the more dignified "Aunt Alva." She was a favorite school teacher in the little town where I grew up. Aunt Alva was also the music teacher, and that only added to my delight of being in her class.

My auntie would draw the most beautiful staff on the blackboard, and then explain the treble and bass clef signs and the notes with great enthusiasm. After one such session, a little red-haired boy at a back desk blurted out with wonder, "Miss Alva, what'll you think of next?"

When I read Philemon, I feel like murmuring, "Paul, what will you think of next?" Of all his amazing requests, the one in this letter takes the cake. He actually wants Philemon to take back a runaway slave and love him as a brother!

He asked this in an era when human life was cheap, gladiators battled wild animals in a blood-soaked arena to the delight of the crowd. It was a time when runaway slaves were hunted down like wild pigs and killed without thought. It was this kind of world for slaves, and yet Paul makes his enormous request of Philemon.

In the small museum at the entrance of the ancient city of Corinth, I remember being moved as I looked at a tall, beautifully sculpted statue of a slave that had once stood atop an upper column of the building that housed the slave market during the days of Paul. That slave market was right across the street from the Bema where Paul defended himself before the authorities of Corinth.

Later in Rome that slave market may have come to Paul's mind as he got to know Onesimus and felt toward him like a father, "whom I have begotten in my bonds." Perhaps being in his own bonds—his slavery to power beyond his control—gave Paul the strong feeling of fatherhood to Onesimus. But as much as he came to love and need Onesimus, Paul knew there was a wrong to be made right with Philemon, his friend in Colossae, who owned Onesimus.

Philemon was a brother in the faith. Paul calls him a brother, partner, dearly beloved, and fellowlaborer. So powerful were the apostle's feelings for both Philemon and Onesimus that he rose to one of his highest peaks of rhetoric in writing some of the most beautiful words in our entire New Testament:

> Wherefore, though I might be much bold in Christ
> to enjoin thee that which is convenient,
> Yet for love's sake I rather beseech thee,
> being such an one as Paul the aged,
> and now also a prisoner of Jesus Christ.
> I beseech thee for my son Onesimus,
> whom I have begotten in my bonds....

Socially, the small letter to Philemon was a bombshell. What a fantastic crack in the culture. What a breakthrough and a sudden light on the abominable practice of slavery that was so taken for granted.

These few verses set me on a quest in my own confusing, media-controlled world. What is real? Where are *my* blind spots? What evil am I taking for granted? How immersed am I in my socially accepted stratum? How insulated am I from people unlike me? And I feel that I need to pray, "Lord, introduce me, perhaps painfully, to the cracks in our culture, where there may be an Onesimus, a slave of some evil, who can be restored through my efforts to full brother status."